Our American Century

★

People Who Shaped the Century

By the Editors of Time-Life Books, Alexandria, Virginia

Contents

★

A Note to Our Readers

Some say history is made by exceptional people who come forward to direct events; others argue that events grow from complex circumstances, mobilizing extraordinary individuals. The editors of People Who Shaped the Century *take no side in this debate. They were content to celebrate the cavalcade of fascinating personalities who, in ways large and small, whether for good or evil or something in between, put their seal on our century. The book includes at least one personality for each year of the century, the chosen year corresponding to a key time in that person's life. Accompanying 18 of the personalities—for example, Frank Lloyd Wright, in 1911—are boxes featuring other notables in the same field of endeavor.*

A happy serendipity emerged as the editors assembled this table of contents: It forms a kind of "class picture" of the century in which we learn that surprisingly disparate figures shared the same slice of time, striding through history side by side. We wouldn't normally associate Louis Armstrong with educational reformer John Dewey, for example, yet a glance to the right shows that they arrived at a significant moment in their lives at virtually the same time. So, too, did such unlikely pairs as Katharine Hepburn and Adolf Hitler, Milton Berle and Mao Zedong, Fidel Castro and fast-food king Ray Kroc.

The table of contents is chronological, with years on the left and page numbers on the right. The titles in italic type identify the boxes featuring associated personalities.

Neil Kagan
Publisher/Managing Editor
Time-Life Books

1900

Sigmund Freud
The Founder of Psychoanalysis

Pictured above at age 16 with his vivacious mother, young Freud drew confidence from the knowledge that he was her "undisputed darling."

Freud practiced in this consulting room in his home, where he lived with his wife and children. Here patients would lie on a couch—soon to be a cliché of psychoanalysis—and say whatever crossed their minds, a process Freud called free association.

As the 20th century dawned, a radical new book appeared that forever changed people's understanding of human behavior. In *The Interpretation of Dreams,* 43-year-old Viennese physician Sigmund Freud argued that dreams offered clues to a swirl of unsettling desires that the conscious mind repressed. Among them was the Oedipus complex, so called for a figure in Greek mythology who unwittingly killed his father and married his mother. Freud detected that complex in his own childhood relationship with his youthful and doting mother and his much older father.

In the Victorian milieu of the time, such suggestions provoked sharp controversy. "People did not believe in my facts and found my theories unsavory," Freud wrote. "Resistance was strong and unrelenting." Much to his surprise, his ideas did better in the land he called "prudish America" than in Europe. By the Roaring '20s, Freudianism had become fashionable among fashionable Americans. People without any complexes to speak of tried to coax them into being by reclining on couches and confiding in practitioners of Freudian theory known as psychoanalysts—or, irreverently, as headshrinkers. Although one critic charged that Freud lived in a "fairyland of dreams among the ogres of perverted sex," his professed aim was to help patients function better by equipping them with a healthy ego that could reconcile the instinctive urges he called the id with the moral inhibitions he termed the superego.

One powerful urge Freud could not repress in himself was smoking. As shown in the portrait at right, made around 1921, he was seldom without a cigar, and he later developed cancer of the jaw, undergoing 33 operations. A confirmed atheist who nonetheless cherished his Jewish heritage, he fled Nazi persecution in his Austrian homeland and emigrated to England in 1938, where he died the following year. His psychoanalytic "talking cure" came to be challenged by rival therapies, but no one who sought to understand the ills of the mind could escape Freud's towering influence.

Harry Houdini

Escape Artist Extraordinaire

Handcuffs, straitjackets, chains, padlocks—these were the tools of the great Harry Houdini, who rocketed to international fame in 1900 during a European tour that saw him slip miraculously out of bindings from London to Moscow. Born Erik Weisz in 1874 in Hungary, he grew up in Wisconsin and, later, New York. At 17 he began doing magic tricks in circuses and sideshows, taking his stage name from Jean Eugène Robert-Houdin, a celebrated French magician. A master of self-promotion, Houdini would perform nearly naked to convince the audience that he possessed nothing that might help him escape —although he often had a concealed key or picklock—and, perhaps more important, to titillate the women in attendance with the sight of his impressive physique.

To build up excitement for his stage shows he would perform well-publicized outdoor feats. One such was the Detroit Bridge Jump: Chained and handcuffed before a crowd on a November day in 1906, he dropped into the frigid Detroit River, surfacing minutes later with restraints in hand. Onstage he thrilled audiences with the Giant Milk Can Escape and, later, the even more dramatic Chinese Water Torture Cell, in which his manacled body was lowered upside down into a small glass-walled chamber filled with water. "I vehemently want to be first," he said of his craft. "I have tortured my body and risked my life only for that."

Houdini died in 1926 from the effects of a ruptured appendix, caused when he invited a young man to test his conditioning by punching him in the stomach and was caught off guard by the blow. His fame was such that in death his name became part of the language as a synonym for someone getting out of an impossible predicament.

Shackled from neck to ankle, Houdini flexes his muscles in a publicity shot that helped lure admirers to his shows.

Guglielmo Marconi

The Father of Radio

Shortly after noon on December 12, 1901, a 27-year old Italian inventor sat in a small room atop a hill in St. John's, Newfoundland, a receiving device held to his ear. Suddenly, in the silence, Guglielmo Marconi (shown below with his Newfoundland wireless) heard three sharp clicks—Morse code for the letter *S*—and a wave of relief and triumph swept over him. The brief signal had traveled through the air all the way from a transmitting station manned by one of Marconi's assistants in southwestern England, more than 2,000 miles away.

Never before had a signal traveled so far without passing through a telegraph wire. Scientists had declared the feat impossible, predicting that radio waves, which move in straight lines, would not reach a distant receiver because of the earth's curvature. As it turned out, the waves were reflected back to earth by the atmosphere, "serenely ignoring," as Marconi put it, the contour of the globe. He had proven the feasibility of worldwide wireless communication.

For his feat Marconi was justly hailed as the father of radio. But others had paved the way. In the 1860s British physicist James Maxwell had postulated the existence of electromagnetic waves, and in the 1880s German scientist Heinrich Hertz had discovered a way to generate them. Marconi, working at home under the stern disapproval of his father, a rich landowner, attached an improved version of Hertz's generator to an outdoor antenna and succeeded in 1895 in transmitting signals to a receiver a mile away. He went on to form his own company and refine his instruments, increasing the range of transmission until it spanned the Atlantic. His work won him the Nobel Prize for physics in 1909 and revolutionized human communication.

1901

Booker T. Washington

Educator and Leader

I n his best-selling 1901 autobiography, *Up From Slavery*, Booker T. Washington wrote that a man's success should be measured "not so much by the position he has reached as by the obstacles which he has overcome." Washington himself could claim success by either standard.

He was born on a Virginia plantation in 1856, the son of a slave woman and an unidentified white man. After the Civil War his family moved to West Virginia, where he attended school while toiling in mines morning and night. At 17 he left home for Hampton Institute, a pioneering black school, where he acquired his lifelong philosophy that hard work and self-discipline were the keys to a decent life for the South's poor, uneducated, and powerless blacks.

In 1881, at the age of 25, Washington took charge of a new black school in Tuskegee, Alabama. Under his leadership, students built the school brick by brick, and Tuskegee Institute eventually won renown for training educators and providing extension programs for the rural poor.

In 1895 Washington captured attention with his "Atlanta Compromise" speech. Delivered in a climate of increasing racial oppression, his message advocated career training and economic betterment rather than academic education and the struggle for equal rights. Such views gave him status among whites as the nation's foremost black spokesman, enabling him to acquire great power in the black community. But he incurred criticism from other black leaders—most notably W. E. B. Du Bois *(page 28)*— who felt Washington was harming his people spiritually and condemning them to permanent underclass status.

Until his death in 1915, Washington, shown below in his Tuskegee office, fought the Du Bois camp. Yet he often pressed for political and judicial advances behind the scenes, advising several presidents on racial issues.

Annie Sullivan and Helen Keller

The Miracle Worker and the Miracle

The most important day I remember in all my life is the one on which my teacher, Anne Mansfield Sullivan, came to me," wrote the blind and deaf Helen Keller in her 1902 autobiography, *The Story of My Life.* That stirring account was as much a tribute to the 22-year-old author as it was to Sullivan *(below right, facing Keller),* who put her pupil in touch with the world.

Robbed of sight and hearing by a fever at 19 months, Keller struggled to communicate through noises and gestures. "I was a phantom living in a no-world," she said. "My inner life . . . was a blank without past, present, or future." Often unable to make herself understood, she threw violent temper tantrums. Just before her seventh birthday, her parents enlisted the help of Sullivan, a graduate of the Perkins Institute for the Blind whose own vision had been impaired by an eye disease.

Sullivan began trying to teach Keller the alphabet by touch. After a month, when Sullivan spelled the word *water* into the child's palm as she held it under a flowing pump, Keller realized suddenly that the strange finger movements represented the names of things, and that they were the key to everything she wanted to learn.

Ascending to literacy, Keller came to consider the date Sullivan entered her life as her "soul's birthday." She went on to achievements unheard of for a person with her disabilities, graduating from Radcliffe in 1904 and emerging as a prolific writer and a tireless advocate for the handicapped.

1902

Enrico Caruso
The Golden Tenor

Born in Naples in 1873 to a family of 20 children, Enrico Caruso started singing in cafés. His first voice teacher compared his early efforts to "wind whistling through a window," but he soon developed a powerful, melodious voice that won him acclaim as the King of Tenors.

"His was the most wonderful tenor I have ever heard," said soprano Nellie Melba, his favorite performing partner. "It had a magnificent ease, and a truly golden richness." In 1902 Caruso crafted a gift for future generations when, during his debut in England, he met Fred Gaisberg, a pioneer in sound recording, and agreed to record 10 arias for a fee of 100 pounds. The following year he sang for the first time at the New York Metropolitan Opera—in Verdi's *Rigoletto;* he would be the Met's leading star for the rest of his life. Among the roles Caruso made his own was the sad clown Canio in Leoncavallo's *I Pagliacci (left).*

1903

Marie and Pierre Curie
Paragons of Mutual Affection and Genius

We had no money, no laboratory and no help," wrote Marie Curie of the brilliant but grueling work for which she and her husband, Pierre, won the Nobel Prize for physics in 1903. That work began in 1896, after their French colleague Antoine-Henri Becquerel, who shared the prize with them, discovered mysterious rays emanating from uranium. Marie, then a 28-year-old graduate student in Paris who had wed Pierre the year before, was riveted by Becquerel's discovery, and not even the birth of her first child, Irène, kept her from pursuing the search for other elements that emitted such rays, which she named radioactivity. Pierre dropped his own studies on magnetism to join her.

Toiling in a shed that was stifling in summer and freezing in winter, the Curies processed two tons of the radioactive ore pitchblende to isolate its elements. "It was killing work, to stir, for hours at a stretch, the boiling matter in a smelting basin," Marie wrote. "In the evening I was broken with fatigue." Both suffered from exposure to radiation, and Marie lost a child, born prematurely. But they succeeded in identifying two new radioactive elements, which they named radium and polonium (for Marie's native Poland). Their work helped confirm that radioactivity was a by-product of decaying atoms, shattering the belief that atoms were indivisible. They also pioneered a treatment for cancer by showing that exposure to radium destroyed tumor cells while causing less harm to healthy tissue. Pierre exposed his arm to radium for several hours to study the damage and the healing process.

Their great scientific partnership ended abruptly in 1906 when Pierre was run over by a horse-drawn cart and died at 47. Although devastated, Marie clung tenaciously to her work and in 1911 became the first scientist to win a second Nobel Prize, this one for chemistry. The Curies' daughter Irène and her husband, Frédéric Joliot-Curie, went on to win their own Nobel Prize, for chemistry, in 1935, a year after Marie's death from radiation-induced leukemia. "Of all celebrated beings," Albert Einstein said of Marie, "[she is] the only one whom fame has not corrupted."

Dedicated to their work, Pierre and Marie Curie relied for both recreation and transportation on their bicycles, which they purchased with wedding-gift money.

1903

Orville and Wilbur Wright

Brothers in Flight

At 10:35 a.m. on December 17, 1903, a 32-year-old Dayton, Ohio, bicycle mechanic named Orville Wright climbed into a contraption he had built with his brother, Wilbur, and prepared to leap into history. Poised atop a dune at Kitty Hawk, on one of the islands that make up North Carolina's Outer Banks, the Wrights' "Flyer" would, they hoped, make the world's first powered heavier-than-air flight. Wilbur, four years older than Orville, recalled that as children the two had "played together, worked together and, in fact, thought together." Neither finished high school, but they had good minds and hands. Wilbur *(far right)* conceived the aircraft, and the mustachioed Orville worked out many of the details.

The brothers came to Kitty Hawk to take advantage of the lift provided by its brisk winds and the cushioning offered by its sands—a crash was never far from their minds. When all was ready, Wilbur saw Orville off with a long,

An updated Flyer piloted by Wilbur Wright sweeps across Manhattan on a 20-mile flight six years after Orville's first 100-foot hop.

heartfelt handshake, "sort of like," one witness observed, "two folks parting who weren't sure they'd ever see one another again." Then with a clatter of its engine the plane lurched forward, accelerated down 40 feet of track laid in the sand, and lifted into the air, bucking and dipping before alighting safely 100 feet away. The epochal deed had lasted only 12 seconds, but humankind was in the air to stay.

By 1909 the Wrights were making extended flights like one over Manhattan *(above)*. Wilbur died of typhoid in 1912, but Orville lived until 1948, having seen transatlantic flights, air warfare, and planes with wingspans longer than the entire distance of that first brave flight at Kitty Hawk.

Dressed here for track, a pugnacious-looking Roosevelt competed in several sports at Harvard.

Roosevelt (center) and his Rough Riders won fame in Cuba charging up San Juan Hill.

Roosevelt stands with naturalist John Muir at Yosemite, one of the national parks he created.

1904

Theodore Roosevelt

A Monumental Leader

D o you know the two most wonderful things I have seen in your country?" declared a visiting English statesman during Theodore Roosevelt's time in the White House. "Niagara Falls and the President of the United States. Both great wonders of Nature!" It was an apt tribute to this monumental figure, a vigorous outdoorsman who overwhelmed political opponents with the force of his convictions.

Born to a wealthy family in New York City in 1858, young Roosevelt lacked only one advantage in life—good health. In his own words "a sickly, delicate boy," he overcame severe asthma through strenuous exercise and eventually excelled at sports. His dashing role as colonel of the Rough Riders in Cuba during the Spanish-American War helped him win nomination as Republican presidential candidate William McKinley's running mate in 1900. He got the nod over the objections of party boss Mark Hanna, who warned prophetically that "there was only one life between this madman and the White House."

Thrust into the presidency when an assassin's bullet struck McKinley down, Roosevelt boldly challenged moneyed interests on behalf of the public by suing to break up corporate monopolies, earning the sobriquet Trust Buster. In 1904 he was returned to the White House by a landslide vote. "Tomorrow I shall come into office in my own right," he reportedly told friends on the eve of his inauguration. "Then watch out for me!"

TR, as he was widely known, increased pressure on those he called "malefactors of great wealth" by targeting John D. Rockefeller's Standard Oil Company for dismemberment and clamping controls on rapacious railroads and unscrupulous meat packers. He was no less forceful abroad, applying his diplomatic maxim, "Speak softly and carry a big stick," by dispatching naval forces to the Colombian province of Panama to support a rebellion, thereby clearing the way for the construction of an American-controlled canal across the isthmus.

In 1912, four years after stepping down as president, Roosevelt bid unsuccessfully for reelection as head of the Progressive, or Bull Moose, Party, campaigning with tireless exuberance *(right)*. When he died in 1919, Vice President Thomas Marshall said, "Death had to take him sleeping, for if Roosevelt had been awake, there would have been a fight."

Einstein poses in 1904 with his first wife, Mileva, and Hans Albert, the elder of his two sons, in Bern, Switzerland, where he worked in the patent office.

Albert Einstein

Theorist of the Atomic Age

In 1905 an obscure Swiss patent clerk stunned the scientific world by publishing several papers that challenged fundamental assumptions about the nature of the universe. The source of such earthshaking theories was a surprise, for few had expected great things of Albert Einstein.

Born in Germany in 1879, Einstein so disliked formal education that at one point he actually quit school. While still in his teens, however, he began to visualize problems of baffling complexity and foresee solutions that he then worked out mathematically. One such exercise, in which he imagined himself moving at the speed of light but frozen in time, contributed to his theory of special relativity, which shattered the long-held belief that time passes at an absolute and unchanging rate. As Einstein proved mathematically in 1905—and as later measurements confirmed—time slows down for an object moving at high speed relative to a fixed point on earth.

Einstein also stated that "mass is merely another form of energy," as expressed in his now famous equation $E = mc^2$ (energy equals mass times the speed of light squared). His conclusions were hard to test— one physicist called them "a theorist's paradise but an experimentalist's hell." When scientists later split the atom and released vast amounts of energy, however, the sobering truth of $E = mc^2$ hit home.

The celebrity that came to him as a result of these assertions did little to change Einstein, an often disheveled figure who went around engrossed in thought and detached from his surroundings. "I have never belonged wholeheartedly to country or state, to my circle of friends, or even to my own family," he once said. His first marriage ended in divorce, and Einstein subsequently wed his cousin Elsa before moving to the United States in 1933 to teach at Princeton University.

Fearing calamity for the world and annihilation for his fellow Jews if Nazi scientists should be the first to unleash the power of the atom, he wrote a letter to President Franklin Roosevelt in 1939 urging that the United States build a nuclear weapon. He remained a pacifist at heart, however, and later reacted with words of warning to the news that Hiroshima had been obliterated by an atomic bomb: "The world is not ready for it."

Einstein gazes pensively out to sea in California while visiting a foundation that funded some of his research. When a crowd gathered to gawk at the world-renowned physicist, he left.

As shown here in the 1930s, Einstein was an avid teacher as well as a theorist. He remained at the Institute for Advanced Study at Princeton until his death in 1955 at the age of 76.

> "I don't know whether anyone will care to examine my heart, but if they do, they will find two words there—'social justice.' For that is what I have believed in and fought for."

Upton Sinclair

Upton Sinclair
Paladin of Reform

It will shake the heart and blow the top off of the industrial tea-kettle," wrote Upton Sinclair of his muck-raking classic, *The Jungle*, a fictional exposé of conditions in the Chicago stockyards. Published in 1906, the bestseller followed a family of Lithuanian immigrants as they struggled to make a living in Packingtown, the city's meat-processing district. Sinclair had witnessed the brutal conditions there and meant to throw light on the plight of the workers. Instead, horrified readers focused on his descriptions of unscrupulous practices in the meat-packing plants, where vermin and diseased animals sometimes became part of the product passed along to consumers. "I aimed at the public's heart," Sinclair *(left)* remarked, "and by accident I hit it in the stomach."

The Jungle touched off an uproar, and Theodore Roosevelt invited Sinclair to the White House. With this entrée the crusading author so pestered Roosevelt on the need for government action that the president pleaded with his publisher, "Tell Sinclair to go home and let me run the country for a while." Nonetheless, Roosevelt launched an investigation that resulted in the passage of the Pure Food and Drug Act and the Meat Inspection Act.

Born in Baltimore in 1878, Sinclair was the product of a genteel family that fell on hard times as a result of his father's alcoholism. A vegetarian who ate mainly brown rice, fresh fruit, celery, and dried milk, he lived to the age of 90 and wrote more than 90 books. He possessed a "combative innocence," as literary critic Alfred Kazin put it, that led him into fights for goals that seemed beyond reach—most notably, his unsuccessful run for the governorship of California during the Depression on a platform that promised to end poverty there. Yet many of the causes he espoused —such as trade unions, the abolition of child labor, and birth control—ultimately won broad public support.

Pablo Picasso
Master of Modernism

His eyes widen, his nostrils flare," observed an admirer who watched Pablo Picasso at work; "he attacks the canvas like a picador sticking a bull." In 1907, at the age of 26, the masterful Spaniard wielded his brush as never before and executed a revolutionary work, *Les Demoiselles d'Avignon (below, right)*. In stark contrast to the shapely nudes of classical art, these ladies were twisted and deformed, as though viewed through a distorting lens from several angles at once.

When Picasso showed the piece to his friends, they were dumbfounded. Fellow artist Georges Braque said that "to paint in such a way was as bad as drinking petrol in the hope of spitting fire." But Picasso, sure of his purpose, weathered the criticism. He knew that by ignoring the es-tablished conventions of beauty and perspective, he had created a new way of looking at the world.

He soon won Braque over to his camp, and together they pioneered the style called cubism. Their purpose was not to mirror the visible world but to break it down into its essential elements and reassemble those parts on canvas. The two artists compared themselves to the Wright brothers; as they saw it, both teams were conducting bold experiments in space.

In art and in life Picasso followed his impulses. "Painting is stronger than I am," he said. "It makes me do what it wants." Ever susceptible to passion, he had a succession of mistresses. He once said that there were "only two kinds of women, goddesses and doormats," and some of his favorites played both roles before he was through with them. He married twice, the last time at 70 to 28-year-old Jacqueline Roque, with whom he lived until his death in 1972, at the age of 91. The prolific artist left behind some 20,000 works and a modernist vision that defined art in the 20th century.

Les Demoiselles d'Avignon

21

Still vigorous at the age of 68, Pablo Picasso uses a flashlight to trace the image of a minotaur— half man, half bull—a mythic figure he identified with.

Vanguard of an Artistic Revolution

Twentieth-century Europe was a hotbed of experimentation in painting and sculpture, led by iconoclasts such as those below.

Around the middle of the century, brash American artistic innovators began to set trends for the rest of the world to follow.

 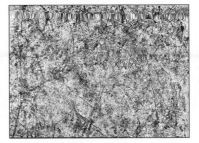

Henri Matisse *In so-called primitivist works like Dance (above), completed in 1909, the French painter Matisse enlivened his spare forms with bold colors and infused modern art with an exuberance that he and his compatriots characterized as joie de vivre.*

Jackson Pollock
Called Jack the Dripper for his technique of dropping paint on canvas to produce compositions like 1950's Lavender Mist (above), Pollock insisted that there was method to his "action painting" and that the result was "no accident."

Marcel Duchamp

A Frenchman who made his second home in New York, Duchamp fashioned everyday objects into "ready-made" artworks like his 1913 Bicycle Wheel (right). He later shocked American audiences by exhibiting a urinal under the title Fountain.

Robert Rauschenberg

Expanding on "ready-made" art, Rauschenberg painted objects to create "combine paintings," like his 1955 signature work Bed (right). "Painting relates to both art and life," he said. "I try to act in the gap between the two."

Constantin Brancusi *The Romanian sculptor Brancusi reduced subjects to their abstract essence. His*

sleek 1928 work Bird in Space (right) sparked a court case when a U.S. Customs official charged that he was trying to avoid import taxes on bronze by calling it art.

Andy Warhol

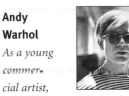 

As a young commercial artist, Warhol recognized the power of the classic images that sold products and fed fantasies. He made creative use of those icons in works like 1962's The Twenty Marilyns (right), which epitomized the Pop Art movement.

In 1896 budding automaker Henry Ford sits proudly at the tiller of his first car, which he built in a shed behind his house in Detroit.

Henry Ford

Pioneer of Mass Production

Everybody wants to be someplace he ain't," asserted Henry Ford. "As soon as he gets there he wants to go right back." The man who catered to that restlessness embodied it himself, leaving his rural Dearborn, Michigan, home in 1879 at age 16 to work in a machine shop in nearby Detroit. He later returned home and tinkered with designs for a tractor before taking a job with the Detroit Edison Company.

Ford devoted his spare time to a project dear to his heart, eventually producing a "horseless carriage" *(left)*. In 1903, when he was 40, he amassed enough capital from investors to found the Ford Motor Company, and in 1908, after a period of mixed success with various models, he introduced his Model T—the car that put America on wheels.

At the dawn of the automobile age many entrepreneurs were producing fine cars, but Ford outstripped them all in one crucial aspect of the business—the manufacturing process. He instituted the assembly line and other mass-production techniques that radically cut costs, making cars affordable to the average family. The secret, in his own words, was "taking the work to the men instead of the men to the work."

Ford built a factory where workers remained in place and bolted on parts as the auto frame rolled by. At a time when other cars were selling for thousands of dollars, the first Model Ts went for a mere $850, and Ford eventually worked that figure down to $360. "Every time I lower the price a dollar," he boasted, "we gain a thousand new buyers." Almost overnight he became the nation's leading carmaker.

Many of Ford's ideas were brilliant, but others betrayed gross ignorance and bigotry. In 1914 he instituted a then-princely minimum pay rate of $5 a day for his employees, but he opposed their efforts to unionize, using goons to assail strikers. He declared that "history is more or less bunk" and published an anti-Semitic newspaper, yet he considered himself an expert on world affairs and campaigned (unsuccessfully) for the U.S. Senate in 1918, prompting the *New York Times,* with biting wit, to observe that his election "would create a vacancy both in the Senate and in the automobile business." By the time he died in 1947, Ford had fallen far out of touch with the times in both his industry and society at large, but no one could deny that his genius had permanently changed the world.

1909

Leo Baekeland

Plastic Man

For manufacturers and consumers alike, the 20th century became the age of plastics. Credit for the birth of this new era could fairly be laid at the feet of one man—a chemist named Leo H. Baekeland, who in 1909 patented the first heat-resistant plastic, which he proudly named Bakelite. There had been earlier plastics, but Baekeland's breakthrough was to produce a material that, once it hardened, would hold its shape even when subjected to high heat.

Born and educated in Belgium, Baekeland came to the United States in 1889 on a postdoctoral fellowship and soon invented a photographic paper that was sensitive to artificial light, making it possible to develop prints indoors. Eastman Kodak bought Baekeland's invention and made him a wealthy man. He took his money and built a laboratory in his home so that he could "enjoy the luxury of not being interrupted in one's favorite work."

There he embarked on the meticulous research that yielded Bakelite, which also proved an effective insulator. Carmakers used it in their ignition systems, and manufacturers molded it into handles for pots and appliances, like the iron at right. Countless ingenious plastics have been developed since, but Baekeland's creation holds pride of place as the catalyst for a new age.

"I hope to remain until I die a post graduate student at that greater school of practical life, which has no fixed curriculum and where no academic degrees are conferred."

Leo H. Baekeland, 1907

Inventors of Everyday Objects

While the new century saw greater advances in science and technology than in all previous human history, people's lives were also changed in ways large and small by practical inventions—everything from automobile starters to pop-up toasters to zippers. Some of these were the brainchildren of trained scientists; others came from original minds sparked by flashes of insight.

King C. Gillette *The handy "Safety Razor" (above) devised by salesman Gillette was advertised as requiring "No Stropping, No Honing." When the blade became dull, it was simply replaced. In 1903, the first year of production, only 51 of the razors were sold, but they soon swept the nation.*

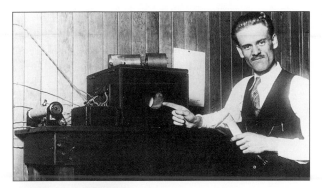

 **Philo T. Farnsworth** *In 1922, when he was just 16, Farnsworth sketched out an idea for television—a plan he fulfilled in 1927 with a camera and receiver of his own design (above). Independently, Vladimir Zworykin developed television for RCA, but Farnsworth is considered the father of TV and even marketed his own set (left).*

Edwin Land *"Why can't I see the pictures now?" asked Land's daughter one day after he snapped her photo. Within hours, the inventor of polarized sunglasses conceived a camera that printed pictures on the spot. Introduced in 1947, the Polaroid Land Camera (above) was an instant sensation.*

George de Mestral *After a 1948 outing, Swiss inventor de Mestral examined under a microscope burrs that stuck to his clothing, spotting minute hooks that clung to loops of thread in the cloth. He mimicked that combination in the fabric he dubbed Velcro (above), introduced in 1957.*

Bill Bowerman *In 1972 track coach Bowerman poured rubber onto a waffle iron and cooked up a new sole for running shoes that was light and flexible and offered ample cushioning. Introduced by Nike, Bowerman's wafflelike sole gave athletes an edge and helped popularize jogging.*

1909

W. E. B. Du Bois
Civil Rights Visionary

Although African American historian and reformer W. E. B. Du Bois considered himself "neither a leader nor an agitator," he refused to sit idly by while his people were "lynched, murdered, and starved." On February 12, 1909, the 100th anniversary of Abraham Lincoln's birthday, he joined with like-minded black activists and liberal whites in founding the National Association for the Advancement of Colored People (NAACP), a pioneering civil rights group that became black America's leading self-help organization.

Born in Massachusetts in 1868, Du Bois was admitted to Harvard, becoming the first of his race to receive a PhD there. No less important to his development, however, were the years he spent preparing for Harvard at Fisk University in Tennessee, where he encountered, on the one hand, what he called a "beautiful world of Black folk" and, on the other, the harsh realities of segregation and lynchings. He came away convinced that blacks must fight for their rights as American citizens and emerged as a sharp critic of Booker T. Washington *(page 10),* who emphasized vocational training at the expense of higher education and the struggle for rights. "We want the constitution of the country enforced," Du Bois insisted. "We want our children educated."

Editor of the NAACP journal *Crisis,* Du Bois (shown below during his long tenure as the organization's only black officer) late in life moved to Ghana, where he died in 1963 at the age of 95, just one day before Dr. Martin Luther King Jr. led 200,000 civil rights demonstrators in a history-making march on Washington, D.C.

Igor Stravinsky
Musical Rebel

In 1910 Russian composer Igor Stravinsky completed one piece that would delight listeners and began work on another that would provoke them to fury. That June his *Firebird,* composed for the Ballets Russes, debuted to rave reviews. Inspired by the romantic music of Stravinsky's mentor, Nikolay Rimsky-Korsakov, it barely hinted at what the 27-year-old had in store for the world. For he was already dreaming up another ballet, but one that would be savage in theme and strident in tone. Entitled *The Rite of Spring,* it dealt with human sacrifice and stirred up a storm of controversy when it was first performed, in Paris in 1913. Audiences rioted, shouting and throwing programs at the performers. Some listeners were overwhelmed by the dissonant score, others were simply appalled. One patron reported that a young man seated behind him "began to beat rhythmically on the top of my head with his fists. My emotion was so great that I did not feel the blows for some time."

Despite the widespread hostile reaction to what one critic called its "ear-splitting discords and ponderous rhythms," *The Rite of Spring* soon came to have a tremendous influence on other composers. Like the radical works of Picasso and other modern artists, it broke with tradition and evoked the raw power of primitivism.

Defying convention came naturally to Stravinsky, pictured here around 1914. The son of an opera basso, he said of his youth that he endured it "waiting for the moment when I could send everyone and everything connected with it to hell." Yet this musical rebel shunned the revolutionaries who seized power in Russia in 1917, settling briefly in Switzerland and then in France. He spent his later years in Hollywood, where he continued to compose, steadfastly refusing offers to write movie scores.

> "I was convinced he was raving mad. . . . such music would certainly cause a scandal."
>
> Conductor Pierre Monteux, on Stravinsky's *Rite of Spring*

1911

Frank Lloyd Wright

Architect Without Peer

The house that took shape on a Wisconsin hillside in 1911 was long and low and made of local sandstone. Its creator, Frank Lloyd Wright, named it Taliesin, Welsh for "shining brow." "Hill and house should live together," he declared, "each the happier for the other."

A draftsman at 18, Wright soon won world fame for his low "prairie-style" houses, with their flowing interior spaces lit through broad expanses of glass. Later structures, like the breathtaking Fallingwater *(right)*, expressed Wright's organic concepts spectacularly and blazed a trail for future generations of American architects.

Harmony was an ideal for Wright, though he had little of it in his scandal-ridden private life, having left his wife and six children to live with a succession of women. Yet he won accolades with such achievements as the Johnson Wax Building in Racine, Wisconsin, whose curved forms and soaring, mushroom-shaped columns composed one of the world's most gloriously humane office spaces.

Late in life he culminated two decades of experiments with curves and arcs by inserting his spiral design for the Guggenheim Museum amid the rectilinear steel-and-glass towers of Manhattan — scoring another triumph and affirming his transcendent position in American architecture.

Wright, shown at left at 19, is pictured at right as the 87-year-old master of Taliesin, where he resided off and on until his death in 1959.

Its concrete terraces cantilevered over a cascading Pennsylvania stream (below), Wright's 1936 creation, Fallingwater, epitomized his belief that a house should be wedded to its environment.

The Century's Architectural Avant-Garde

Like Frank Lloyd Wright, the architects profiled here expressed new visual principles and helped chart the future of building design.

Le Corbusier *Considered the architectural counterpart of Picasso, Le Corbusier (born Charles-Édouard Jeanneret) fused an "emotional relationship" with rough, natural materials in designing the chapel at Ronchamp above, with its masonry walls and a roof that resembles a nun's coif.*

Ludwig Mies van der Rohe *Believing that "less is more," the German-born Mies van der Rohe designed sleek and simple structures of steel and glass like the 38-story Seagram Building (left) in New York City, which in the 1950s became a template for future skyscrapers.*

Louis I. Kahn *Playing off principles of light, form, and power, Kahn used stark, geometric shapes, as shown above in the complex of buildings he designed for the Salk Institute, completed in 1965 in La Jolla, California.*

Eero Saarinen *Always willing to experiment, the Finnish-born Saarinen felt that "an architect must have a combination of sensitivity and crust." His design for Washington's Dulles International Airport, with its canopy-like roof, completed in 1962, is a monument to this philosophy.*

Robert Venturi *With his wife and partner, Denise Scott Brown, Venturi in the 1960s launched the postmodernist movement with his own maxim, "Less is a bore." Their Sainsbury Wing of the National Gallery in London (above) reflects an earlier, more intricate neoclassical period.*

Frank Gehry *Approaching each of his buildings as a "sculptural object," Gehry designed the Guggenheim Museum in Bilbao, Spain, in 1998, with a series of ribbonlike, curved shapes clad in titanium. It has been called one of the most important buildings of the century.*

Andrew Carnegie

Peerless Master of the Art of Giving

When he was 33 years old and had yet to begin earning millions from steelmaking, the budding industrial titan Andrew Carnegie wrote a note to himself: "No idol more debasing than the worship of money." True to this sentiment, Carnegie ended up giving away a large part of his fortune. In 1911, at the age of 75, he donated $125 million to create an educational foundation, the Carnegie Corporation of New York—just one of many causes he supported.

Born in Scotland, Carnegie came to America at the age of 12 after his father, a cottage weaver, lost his livelihood to machine looms. The family settled near Pittsburgh, and Andrew went to work as a factory hand, earning less than 25 cents a day. Bright and ambitious, he soon landed a better job in a telegraph office and caught the eye of a railroad executive, who hired him as his secretary and propelled him up the corporate ladder.

At 30 Carnegie went out on his own, investing in various enterprises before focusing on steel. As controlling shareholder of the Carnegie Steel Company, he plowed profits back into new technologies and bought up mines, mills, ships, and railroads so that he could outproduce and underprice the competition. In 1901 his exasperated rivals, led by financier J. P. Morgan, bought out his company and folded it into U.S. Steel. Carnegie's share of the proceeds was a staggering $225 million.

The settlement left him free to play golf *(right)* and pursue his charitable goals. When he died in 1919 at 84, he left a huge fortune to his heirs. But he had given away even more—a total of $350 million, part of which went to endow some 3,000 free public libraries around the world, perhaps the greatest legacy of a philanthropist who wrote, "The man who dies thus rich, dies disgraced."

> "Pity the poor millionaire, for the way of the philanthropist is hard."
>
> Andrew Carnegie, 1913

Irving Berlin

America's Music Man

When a 23-year-old former singing waiter who called himself Irving Berlin sat down at a piano in 1911, he was hoping to add to a string of modest songwriting successes. Instead, in his unschooled, one-finger style, he plinked out a blockbuster—"Alexander's Ragtime Band." Berlin went on to compose hundreds of hits, including such standards as "White Christmas," "God Bless America," and "Someone to Watch Over Me." Said one music publisher, "It must be hell being Irving Berlin. The poor guy's his own toughest competition."

Born Israel Baline, he had arrived in the United States with his family in 1893 after his father, a cantor, decided they had to flee anti-Jewish pogroms in Russia. He spent his youth in poverty on New York's Lower East Side, singing for coins in saloons. His education was minimal and his musical training nonexistent, but he had a knack for catchy lyrics and melodies and a genius for touching emotional chords.

In 1917, the year the U.S. entered the Great War, Berlin was drafted into the army *(right)* at the relatively advanced age of 29. There he wrote a musical revue, *Yip, Yip, Yaphank,* for his fellow soldiers that became a Broadway hit. In years to come, he composed many other smash musicals for stage and screen, including *Annie Get Your Gun, Top Hat,* and *Holiday Inn.* When Berlin died at 101, fellow composer Jerome Kern summed up his prolific career: "Irving Berlin has no place in American music; he *is* American music."

David Sarnoff

A Columbus of Communications

The dots and dashes coming over the airwaves signaled a calamity: "SS *Titanic* ran into iceberg, sinking fast." In the right spot to receive the dread message that night of April 14, 1912, was a 20-year-old wireless operator named David Sarnoff. For four years Sarnoff had been communicating with ships at sea, first at a station in Nantucket *(above)* and now in Manhattan, but he had never heard anything like this signal, relayed from the North Atlantic in Morse code by shipboard radio operators. This was news that would rivet the attention of all America—indeed the world—and for the next 72 hours Sarnoff stayed at his post, providing fresh reports of the unfolding tragedy.

Sarnoff was a Russian immigrant who had taught himself Morse and gone to work at 15 for the Marconi Wireless Telegraph Corporation. Thanks to his performance during the *Titanic* disaster, he was promoted to management. In 1915 he sent his boss a memo urging that the company capitalize on recent experiments in broadcasting the human voice and build a "radio music box" to bring entertainment and news to listeners at home. After World War I the company, now the Radio Corporation of America (RCA), acted on his advice, and the "music boxes" sold like wildfire.

Short and burly and a hard-driving businessman, Sarnoff continued his innovative ways as general manager and later president of RCA. In 1926 he bought up dozens of local radio stations and formed the first major network, the National Broadcasting Company (NBC), a subsidiary of RCA. Despite the Depression he invested in television and introduced the new medium at the New York World's Fair in 1939. "Now at last we add sight to sound," he announced on the initial broadcast. In the 1950s, under his prodding, RCA researchers developed a compatible color TV system, helping NBC keep abreast of the competition.

Sarnoff stayed at the helm of RCA until 1970, a year before his death at age 80. "In a big ship sailing in an uncharted sea," he once said of the business he built, "one fellow needs to be on the bridge. I happen to be that fellow."

1913

Woodrow Wilson

The Professor as President

God ordained that I should be the next President of the United States," declared a self-righteous Woodrow Wilson before his inauguration in 1913. He perhaps had some justification for fancying himself divinely chosen, having reached the pinnacle of power just three years after leaving a lifelong career as an academic for the political arena. Elected governor of New Jersey in 1910, Wilson claimed the Democratic presidential nomination in 1912 on the 46th ballot, then won the election in November with less than half the popular vote after Theodore Roosevelt's third-party bid split the opposition. Some called it luck, but Wilson saw it as Providence.

Preaching from the political pulpit came naturally to Wilson, born in Virginia in 1856 to a Presbyterian minister who imbued him with a faith as powerful as his intellect. Before running for office, he excelled as a teacher and scholar and served as president of Princeton University. In person, however, Wilson lacked the common touch. Even when playing to crowds *(right),* he seemed aloof. Shaking his hand, one journalist wrote, was like grasping a "pickled mackerel in brown paper." And although he entered the White House with a reputation as a progressive, he instituted harsh Jim Crow policies in federal employment, segregating black workers and sweeping out southern blacks hired by previous administrations.

Operating with the certitude of one guided by God's hand, Wilson met with triumph and tragedy in his second term. His pro-British inclinations, combined with German U-boat attacks on U.S. shipping, led him to abandon neutrality in the First World War. "The world must be made safe for democracy," he told Congress in 1917 when calling for troops.

After U.S. forces helped turn the tide and Germany sued for peace, he went to Paris to hammer out the Treaty of Versailles, which called for a League of Nations to prevent future conflicts. The treaty was God's work, he insisted, but the Senate refused to ratify it, fearing foreign entanglements. Wilson would not consider compromise and set out across the country in 1919 to rally public support, but suffered a stroke that left him partially paralyzed and dependent on his wife, Edith, for the rest of his term. A friend who visited him before he died in 1924 likened him to Isaiah—a prophet whose vision of a new order went unfulfilled in his lifetime.

At the Washington Senators' opening game in 1916 Woodrow Wilson keeps up a presidential custom by throwing out the first ball.

Banned from speaking publicly in Boston in 1929, Sanger dramatized the injustice by having her lips sealed with tape, then writing out her lecture on a blackboard.

Margaret Sanger
Crusader for Reproductive Rights

Margaret Sanger was on a mission. In her youth she had seen her mother weakened by the strain of giving birth to 11 children. Later, while raising three children of her own, the fiery, red-haired Sanger worked as a nurse in one of New York's worst slums, where women routinely bore 10 or more babies and begged her for contraceptives in the hope of breaking the cycle of pregnancy and poverty. After one young mother died from a self-induced abortion, Sanger vowed to improve the lot of women whose miseries were "as vast as the sky."

In 1914 she founded *The Woman Rebel,* a magazine whose stated goal was to "stimulate women to think for themselves and to build up a conscious fighting character." Sanger used the magazine to launch her own fight for "birth control," a term she coined, by promising readers information about contraceptives—at a time when even married couples could not legally obtain them. In August of that year she was indicted for breaking federal obscenity laws by distributing information on birth control through the mail. Those charges were later dropped, but further prosecutions awaited her. In 1916, she again defied the law by opening the nation's first birth-control clinic in a poor section of Brooklyn. Police raided the facility, and Sanger spent 30 days in jail.

Over the next two decades Sanger would be arrested eight times while working unceasingly to change the laws she was accused of violating. In 1921 she founded the organization that became the Planned Parenthood Federation of America. Her efforts finally paid off in the 1930s, when court rulings upheld the distribution of contraceptives and birth-control information. At her death in 1966 she was hailed by a colleague for persuading "America and the world that control of conception is a basic human right."

George Washington Carver
Agricultural Innovator

Southern farmers were in despair. Cotton, ravaged by the boll weevil around 1900, had failed them and had sucked the life out of their soil. Yet they were little inclined to listen when a black agricultural scientist urged them to replenish the earth and beat the boll weevil by planting peanuts, sweet potatoes, and soybeans. "Nothing that grows that easy can be any good," was the general opinion.

But George Washington Carver was a master publicist, and in 1915 he staged an exhibit at the Macon County, Alabama, fair that dramatically showcased the crops he was promoting and a cornucopia of foods that could be prepared from them. After years of such efforts on his part, southern farmers began growing peanuts. Carver devised more than a hundred peanut recipes and eventually developed ways to make more than 300 products from the plant. Over the next 20 years the peanut transformed the southern economy.

The man behind this agricultural bonanza had been born a slave and had homesteaded briefly as a young man before attending Iowa State College and earning a master's degree in botany. In 1896 Booker T. Washington *(page 10)* invited him to chair the agriculture department at Tuskegee Institute, where he remained as head of agricultural research *(inset)* until his death in 1943. His work made him one of the most celebrated African Americans of his day, but Carver deflected credit for his accomplishments, claiming that his ideas came "like a direct revelation from God."

*By turns imperti-
nent, mincing, and
artfully clumsy,
Charlie Chaplin re-
veals three sides of
the Little Tramp, the
character that made
him one of the great
stars of silent film.*

Charlie Chaplin

Comic Genius of the Silent Era

Covering his laughing mouth, gazing in shy adoration at a pretty girl, or delivering a kick to an adversary, the mustachioed little man in oversize pants and a derby hat elevated slapstick to an art form. In the 1915 film *The Tramp*, Charlie Chaplin's talent for simultaneously communicating both humor and pathos made the title character one of the most beloved figures of the century. Chaplin's timeless creation was, in the words of the *New York Times*, a "harassed but gallant Everyman, capriciously knocked about by life, but not so utterly battered that he did not pick himself up in the hope that the next encounter would turn out better."

The origins of the character lay in Chaplin's London childhood. Born in 1889 to a small-time actress mother and an alcoholic music-hall comedian father, he spent his early years in shabby rented rooms, poorhouses, and an orphanage. Gifted with physical grace and a quick wit, he left school at age 10 to go on the British vaudeville circuit, and in 1913 American movie producer Mack Sennett signed him to his Keystone Company.

From then on, Chaplin's fame and fortune grew exponentially. By age 26 he was earning a prodigious $670,000 a year and boasted, with some justice, "I am known in parts of the world by people who have never heard of Jesus Christ." In 1919 he joined with director D. W. Griffith and top stars Douglas Fairbanks and Mary Pickford to found United Artists. There he became the first actor to control every aspect of his films, from directing to editing. After talking pictures were introduced in the late 1920s, he continued to play the Little Tramp without dialogue in classics like *City Lights*, but he retired the character when the market for silent films finally dried up.

Chaplin was as controversial as he was popular. The press made much of his passionate attachments to teenage girls—three of whom he married. And in 1952, after visiting England, he was denied reentry to the United States because of his leftist political views. But 20 years later, all was forgiven when the legendary star returned to Hollywood to receive a special Academy Award and an ovation from his peers. Accepting the Oscar, the emotional Chaplin was all but speechless. "Words seem so futile, so feeble," he said—a fitting epilogue for a master of silent expression.

John Dewey

Champion of Progressive Education

Although he was a shy, rumpled philosophy professor whose lectures sometimes put listeners to sleep, John Dewey roused the nation in 1916 with his book *Democracy and Education,* which criticized authoritarian teaching methods and urged that students be allowed to think for themselves. Dewey, shown below shortly after he joined the faculty of Columbia University in 1904 at age 45, launched a progressive-education movement that favored free inquiry over lessons and drills. Though critics complained that he placed too much emphasis on personal development and too little on book learning, his ideas transformed American education.

Louis Armstrong

Jazz Virtuoso and Ambassador to the World

Jazz and I grew up side by side," said Louis Armstrong. Born in New Orleans in 1901, young "Satchmo" (short for "satchel mouth," in reference to his ample kisser) absorbed the intoxicating rhythms of the city, where black musicians cooked up a hot new offering called jazz in steamy nightclubs with names like Funky Butt Hall. At age 12 he learned to play the cornet. By 1917 he had formed his own combo, working in dives and on riverboats until his idol and mentor, trumpeter Joe "King" Oliver, invited him to join his Chicago band. There Armstrong's career took off.

Delivering sublime harmonies and subtle phrasings and hitting notes no other trumpeter had ever reached, Armstrong singlehandedly transformed jazz from mere dance music into an art form. His blistering horn solos and "scat" vocals made him a sensation. "I went mad with the rest of the town," recalled one musician. "I tried to walk like him, talk like him, eat like him, sleep like him." Armstrong later toured the world and performed in movies like *Pennies From Heaven (left)*. Audiences loved "Pops," as he was called, and the feeling was mutual. "The music ain't worth nothing if you can't lay it on the public," he said a few years before his death in 1971. "What you're there for is to please the people."

Jazz Groundbreakers

The music that came of age with Louis Armstrong continued to evolve as innovative composers and performers moved from swing to bebop to cool jazz and beyond.

Duke Ellington *A bandleader and composer whose fame began in 1927 at Harlem's Cotton Club, Ellington was the original King of Swing, bringing elegance and sophistication to jazz with big-band classics like "Mood Indigo" and "Take the A Train."*

Charlie Parker *In the 1940s Parker's complex melodies and breathless improvisation on the alto sax set jazz on a new path—bebop. Parker and his partner, trumpeter Dizzy Gillespie, demanded and won recognition as artists rather than entertainers.*

Thelonious Monk *The foremost composer of modern jazz, pianist Monk took bebop to the limit, unsettling listeners with rhythmic twists and harmonic turns. In time, audiences embraced works like "Round Midnight."*

Miles Davis *After playing with Parker and Gillespie in the late '40s, trumpeter Davis pioneered a more controlled approach called cool jazz in the '50s and later fused jazz with rock.*

John Coltrane *A charismatic saxophonist, Coltrane soloed with both Davis and Monk and changed the course of jazz in the late '50s when he evolved a style in which the notes ran together to form "sheets of sound."*

1917

Vladimir Ilich Lenin
Czar of Communism

> "In a state worthy of the name there is no liberty. The people want to exercise power, but what on earth would they do with it if it were given to them?"

Vladimir Ilich Lenin, July 1918

Shown here at age four with his sister Olga, Lenin grew up comfortably in a middle-class home.

The balding middle-aged Russian racing by rail across wartime Germany to his homeland in the spring of 1917 was dressed deceptively in an plain business suit. But his high, furrowed brow and piercing eyes revealed a man of uncommon intellect and fierce resolve. Lenin, observed Maxim Gorky, had a mind with "the cold glitter of steel shavings."

His return after a long exile marked a turning point in a career that would shake the world. Born Vladimir Ilich Ulyanov in 1870, he had been little affected in his youth by the political unrest roiling Russia. But all that changed in 1887, when his older brother was hanged for plotting against the czar. Embittered, young Ulyanov embraced the teachings of Karl Marx, who asserted that industrialization would lead inevitably to a revolution by oppressed workers—the proletariat—against their capitalist masters. Agrarian Russia had only a small working class, but Ulyanov hoped to hasten things by giving it a push. In 1895 he was arrested for his underground activities, and in 1897 he was sent to Siberia for three years. Afterward, he fled Russia under his new revolutionary nom de guerre, Lenin.

In exile, he became the leader of a dissident faction of the Marxist Russian Social Democratic Party. Since childhood, he had enjoyed making up games and changing the rules as he went along, and he applied that same manipulative approach to revolutionary politics. He snatched for his breakaway group the name Bolshevik ("majority"), leaving his less radical opponents to passively accept the label Menshevik ("minority"). In truth, Lenin's "majority" party was tiny and conspiratorial.

By 1917, a failing Russian economy coupled with devastating war losses had undermined Czar Nicholas II. His regime collapsed in March and was succeeded by a provisional democratic government that vowed to continue fighting. Lenin hurried home with the assistance of German officials, who, knowing of his contempt for the war, hoped he would seize power.

Lenin did just that in November with a perfectly timed Bolshevik coup that swept aside the faltering provisional government. After agreeing to humiliating peace terms with Germany, he won a savage civil war against counterrevolutionary Russian forces and imposed his Communist regime on the nation, at terrible cost. By the time of his death in 1924, he had fastened his iron grip on Russia as surely as any czar.

As head of the recently formed Communist state, Lenin reviews troops with several of his top commanders in Moscow's Red Square in 1918.

Captain Eddie Rickenbacker leans jauntily against a Swiss-built Nieuport 28, which he flew against the Germans.

Eddie Rickenbacker

America's Flying Ace

I have probably cheated the Grim Reaper more than any other man," speculated Eddie Rickenbacker, the tough-talking loner who brought down 26 enemy planes to become America's top ace during World War I. For his greatest exploit—challenging seven aircraft in a dogfight in 1918 and downing two—he received the Medal of Honor.

Rickenbacker was 26 when the United States entered the fray in 1917 and the call for volunteers went out. He felt sure that he had the makings of a great aerial dogfighter. Like the Wright brothers, he had dropped out of school in his native Ohio and later found work as a mechanic, but he had gone on to become one of the leading racecar drivers in the nation by the age of 20. He tried to persuade the U.S. Army to form a fighter squadron composed entirely of racing drivers. Failing that, he enlisted in the army as a driver but soon transferred to flight school, from which he graduated in just 17 days.

In 1918 the tough, unpolished Rickenbacker joined the 94th Aero Pursuit Squadron in France. His college-educated fellow pilots at first made him feel like an outcast, but he quickly won their respect with his deliberate, lethal approach to combat. One morning before dawn, he flew alone 20 miles into enemy territory. Slowing his Nieuport to an almost noiseless glide over a German airstrip, he set his sights on a plane that was just taking off. "As the distance closed to 50 yards," he later wrote, "I saw my tracer bullets piercing the back of the pilot's seat." Though Rickenbacker's right wing was severely damaged when he pulled up, he was able to nurse the plane back to base. Later, with his fifth kill, he became America's second ace, and a few weeks after that he was promoted to commanding officer of the squadron.

Captain Eddie, as he was popularly nicknamed after the war, went on to a long and eventful career, first in automaking and then in civil aviation, becoming president of Eastern Airlines in 1938 and leading it to prosperity. He suffered near-fatal injuries in an Eastern crash in 1941, and the following year, on an inspection trip for the secretary of war, his plane went down in the Pacific, and he passed 23 days adrift on a raft. Late in life, he calculated that he had survived 134 brushes with death. "It is the easiest thing in the world to die," he said. "The hardest is to live."

John Maynard Keynes

Prophet of Deficit Spending

In June 1919 a British delegate to the Paris Peace Conference talks quit in disgust, warning that the harsh terms of the Versailles treaty would strangle the German economy, with dire consequences. Many dismissed John Maynard Keynes's argument, set forth in his book *The Economic Consequences of the Peace,* but events bore him out. During the Depression Keynes proposed that nations "spend their way back to prosperity" by cutting taxes and boosting expenditures, an idea that became government policy on both sides of the Atlantic. When made a director of the Bank of England in 1941, he said, "Orthodoxy has at last caught up with me." He remained a free spirit, however, saying his one regret was that he had not drunk more champagne.

John L. Lewis

Feisty Battler for the Workingman

In the 40 years that John L. Lewis *(left)* ran the United Mine Workers (UMW), he was worshiped by many and hated by others but ignored by no one. Imperious, bombastic, ready to defy even presidents of the United States, this coal-mining son of a Welsh immigrant miner began a rapid ascent through the UMW hierarchy in his late 20s and at age 40—in 1920—became president of the entire union.

Lewis changed the course of the American labor movement during the '30s. He made sure that New Deal legislation contained language guaranteeing workers the right to organize and bargain collectively. Then he helped miners exercise that right, tripling UMW membership.

In 1935, recognizing that workers in industry generally were unskilled or semi-skilled, not craftsmen, he broke with the craft-oriented American Federation of Labor and created a new union—eventually to be called the Congress of Industrial Organizations (CIO)—which was open to most workers in various industries. By 1938 he had won bloody organizing battles in steel, automaking, and other industries, and his influence was at its peak. Nevertheless, he gave up the leadership of the CIO and devoted the last decades of his life solely to his beloved miners. "You need men and I have all the men," he told mine operators in 1949, "and now I ask, 'What am I bid?'"

Legendary Figures of Organized Labor

Heroes and one antihero, they spoke for workers—often contending against titans of industry in an arena where violence was no stranger.

Mother Jones *This turn-of-the-century "Miners' Angel," Mary Harris Jones, used a sharp tongue to shame bosses on behalf of miners and other toilers—including children doing grueling and dangerous millwork.*

A. Philip Randolph *After founding the Brotherhood of Sleeping Car Porters in 1925, Randolph went on to win an end to racial exclusion and segregation in the defense industry and the armed forces.*

Walter Reuther *Although battered by Ford goons in 1937, Reuther never faltered in championing labor. He led the United Automobile Workers and fought for many causes, including civil rights, healthcare, and housing.*

Jimmy Hoffa *Felony convictions and mob ties shadowed Hoffa and his Teamsters Union. He was a dominating presence until his sudden disappearance in 1975, which is still a mystery.*

Cesar Chavez *Hispanic migrant laborers endured dismal conditions before Chavez started the United Farm Workers in 1966, eventually winning for them health benefits and better wages.*

1921

Mohandas Gandhi
Nonviolent Warrior Against Imperialism

Nothing in the early life of Mohandas Gandhi, born in 1869 near Bombay, hinted at his extraordinary future. He was a dutiful but shy child who did only average work in school, as an early report card attests: "Good at English, fair in Arithmetic and weak in Geography; conduct very good, bad handwriting." Gandhi went on to study law in London and entered practice in South Africa *(inset)*. But he was shocked by the racism he witnessed and experienced there, and he began agitating on behalf of the oppressed Indian population, using a tactic that reflected his inner self—nonviolent resistance. By the time he returned home in 1914, he had committed himself to a life of purity based on fasting, celibacy, manual labor, and self-reliance, which he exhibited by making cloth on a spinning wheel. He had also, by now, become a hero to India's millions, who called him Mahatma—"Great Soul."

Taking the helm of the Indian National Congress in 1921, he initiated a series of campaigns aimed at forcing Great Britain to relinquish control of his homeland. The dominant feature of these campaigns was a boycott of British products, businesses, and courts to protest laws allowing suspected dissidents to be imprisoned without trial. He later led a 200-mile march to protest a tax on salt. More than 60,000 marchers were imprisoned, and Gandhi, named *Time* magazine's Man of the Year in 1931, won the attention of the world.

In the 1930s Winston Churchill dismissed him with such terms as "seditious," "half-naked," and "fakir," and asserted that India would forever be part of the empire. Yet two years after the end of World War II, a weary Britain finally relented, granting independence to the subcontinent but splitting it into a Hindu India and a Muslim Pakistan. Simmering tensions between the rival religions boiled over into murderous rioting, and Gandhi went on a fast until leaders of both sides agreed to stop the slaughter. The violence claimed a final victim, however, when a Hindu fanatic shot Gandhi himself in January 1948. "Our light has gone out," Pandit Jawaharlal Nehru, India's first prime minister, said, "but the light that shone in this country was no ordinary light. For a thousand years that light will be seen in this country, and the world will see it."

Gandhi reads near his spinning wheel in 1946. He advocated a simple village economy for India, believing that industrialization and modern technology were corrosive to the human spirit.

James Joyce

A Voyager Into Rarefied Literary Territory

Brilliant, proud, and chafing bitterly under what he saw as the oppressive ways of his homeland, James Joyce quit Ireland at 22. Yet his ties to Dublin, where he was born in 1882 and whose heart he referred to as "the heart of all the cities of the world," remained strong.

He wrote about it in all his works, including *Ulysses,* his masterpiece, which appeared in France in 1922 and was banned as obscene in the U.S. until 1934. Patterned on Homer's epic, it recounts in utter frankness and stream-of-consciousness style one day in the life of an advertising salesman named Leopold Bloom, his wife Molly, and Stephen Dedalus, also the hero of Joyce's 1916 book, *A Portrait of the Artist as a Young Man.*

The *New York Times* called *Ulysses* the "most important contribution that has been made to fictional literature in the twentieth century"—but predicted that no more than "a few intuitive, sensitive visionaries" would understand it. "The average intelligent reader will glean little or nothing from it . . . save bewilderment and a sense of disgust."

In 1939 Joyce, shown at left in a picture taken while he was living in Paris, published one last fictional view of Dublin, *Finnegans Wake,* a phantasmagoric flow of dreams rendered in dense, punning language. He died two years later—poor, nearly blind, but universally acclaimed as a literary giant.

Masters of 20th-Century Literary Innovation

Tied to Joyce and to one another as colleagues or friends, these writers nonetheless each found a distinctive way to break new ground with their words.

Ezra Pound *Cutting to the bone with austere word pictures, Pound inspired a new style of "imagist" poetry. But politics intervened: Accused of treason for pro-Fascist broadcasts he made from Italy during World War II, he was punished by being committed to a U.S. mental institution.*

T. S. Eliot *Poetry was never the same after Eliot inaugurated the modernist era with his "free verse," breaking from rhyme but holding to a discipline of rhythms. His vignettes of contemporary life touched themes of cultural decay and spiritual regeneration.*

Virginia Woolf *Using an impressionistic style that evoked Joyce but was uniquely hers, Woolf built stories on the innermost thought-life of her characters. The turmoil in these tales echoed her own; in 1941, at age 59, she committed suicide by walking into the ocean and drowning.*

Samuel Beckett *Seeking to convey ideas of eternal "nothingness," Beckett went for the unconventional by challenging language itself and even employing silence in his novels and plays. Despite the dark nature of his work, he was noted for personal tranquillity.*

1923

Henry Luce
Builder of a Magazine Empire

Young Henry Luce *(inset),* a man in a hurry, was perhaps predisposed to hit upon the name *Time* for the weekly newsmagazine he founded with longtime friend Briton Hadden in 1923. Their prospectus linked the title to a great mission: "People are uninformed because no publication has adapted itself to the time which busy men are able to spend on simply keeping informed."

Nor did the stodgy daily press of the era give much space to medicine, art, education, religion, or other newsworthy aspects of everyday life. Luce and Hadden divided their magazine into departments devoted to such topics, then filled each one with terse, sassy articles that, according to Luce, were "either titillating or epic or starkly, supercurtly factual."

Luce managed the business side at first, then assumed editorial command as well after Hadden died in 1929. The following year, despite the Depression, he scored another success with the launch of *Fortune,* a monthly magazine about business—"the distinctive expression of the American genius," he said. His next brainstorm was the pictorial weekly *Life,* one of the most popular magazines ever published. Begun in 1936, *Life* had a circulation of more than two million within three years.

Insatiably curious, enormously influential, and unapologetically opinionated—"Show me a man who claims he is objective and I'll show you a man with illusions," he once said—Luce was a passionate Republican, an archenemy of Communism, and a herald of America's role as "the first modern, technological, prosperous, humane and reverent civilization." His company, Time Inc., pioneered film documentaries, acquired radio and television stations, and published books, but magazines remained his great love. The last he started, a weekly called *Sports Illustrated,* appeared in 1954.

Henry Luce, shown here in 1944, created the world's most influential stable of magazines. Four inaugural issues appear below.

George Gershwin

Marriage Broker for Musical Traditions

Music reached a crossroads in a New York concert hall on February 12, 1924. In attendance were Igor Stravinsky, Sergey Rachmaninoff, and other classical musicians. Onstage, bandleader Paul Whiteman led 23 instrumentalists, including 25-year-old pianist George Gershwin. Six years earlier Gershwin had been working as a lowly try-out pianist on Tin Pan Alley. Then Al Jolson made a hit of his "Swanee," and Gershwin was in the big time. Now the audience listened raptly as he played a 15-minute-long "jazz concerto" he had written at Whiteman's request. Titled *Rhapsody in Blue,* it married jazz and blues idioms to classical strains, and the union was a happy one: A recording made soon afterward sold a million copies. More important, its success made serious musicians the world over take notice of American popular music.

Gershwin—who the *New York Times* later said "was to music what F. Scott Fitzgerald was to prose"—went on to write, with his lyricist brother Ira, many Broadway musicals, but he reserved much of his enormous creative energy for such hybrids as the 1935 "folk opera" *Porgy and Bess.* In 1937, while he was performing, his mind suddenly went blank. He died of a brain tumor a few months later, just 38 years old.

> "Jazz I regard as an American folk music; not the only one, but a very powerful one."
>
> George Gershwin

George Gershwin, shown above in a portrait made in 1928 by the famed photographer Edward Steichen, composed his "jazz concerto" Rhapsody in Blue in three weeks.

1924

Joseph Stalin

Paranoid Author of a Blood-Drenched Tyranny

> "Only on the bones of the oppressors can the people's freedom be founded—only the blood of the oppressors can fertilize the soil for the people's self-rule."
>
> Joseph Stalin, 1905

Soviet founding father Vladimir Lenin had decidedly mixed feelings about his revolutionary underling, Joseph Stalin. But illness had loosened Lenin's hold on the reins of power, and by the time he died in 1924, the man he called a "coarse, brutish bully" had gained control of the Communist Party's day-to-day business. In the political jockeying that followed, Stalin would outmaneuver every rival.

He was born Iosif Vissarionovich Dzhugashvili in Georgia in 1879, the son of an alcoholic shoemaker who regularly beat him. He briefly attended a seminary but was expelled for radicalism and in 1901 joined an underground socialist group. His activities as an agitator, pamphleteer, and organizer of bank robberies cost him seven years in various prisons, but he won Lenin's attention and rose to the upper ranks of the party.

Once in power Stalin ruthlessly collectivized Soviet agriculture—starving or "liquidating" 10 million peasants in the process—and imposed industrialization by decree. In the late '30s he launched a series of "purges" in which millions of real or imagined opponents were executed or died in brutally harsh prison camps in Siberia. He relished the purges, confiding to a comrade, "To choose one's victim, to prepare one's plan minutely, to slake an implacable vengeance, and to go to bed—there is nothing sweeter in the world."

In Adolf Hitler, he seemed to meet his match for treachery. Having signed a nonaggression pact with the Nazi leader in 1939, he was stunned when Germany attacked in mid-1941. The invaders were finally overcome, but only at the cost of unimaginable suffering by the Russian people. As the war wound down, Stalin, ignoring protests from his Western allies, installed puppet regimes in the eastern European nations he had "liberated" from the Nazis, setting the stage for the Cold War.

He was reportedly planning another purge when he died in 1953. His minions mourned him—"Stalin's name is boundlessly dear to our party, to the Soviet people, to the workers of the world," said the Kremlin—but the truth was known: He was a monster of historic proportions.

A 1910 police file includes photos of Stalin and a list of his physical peculiarities—facial scarring by smallpox, a shortened and stiffened left arm, and two toes on his left foot that were fused together.

In the Kremlin office that he rarely left, Stalin works beneath a portrait of Karl Marx (opposite).

Margaret Mead's college graduation portrait reveals a small vanity: It shows her without her spectacles.

"We must recognize that beneath the superficial classifications of sex and race the same potentialities exist, recurring generation after generation, only to perish because society has no place for them."

Margaret Mead, *Male and Female*, 1948

1925

Margaret Mead
Popularizer of Anthropology

Not long before graduating from college, Margaret Mead announced to friends, "I'm going to be famous some day and I'm going to be known by my own name." The eldest child in a family of freethinking academics, Mead took her first anthropology course in her senior year at New York's Barnard College, where her professor warned that the world's primitive societies were in danger of being swept away by the advancing tide of civilization. "That settled it for me," said Mead. "Anthropology had to be done *now*."

In 1925, as a newly minted doctor of anthropology, she took her first step toward the fame she sought, setting sail for the Samoan island of Pago Pago, a lone white woman bent on studying the culture of a primitive tribe. Obstacles to Mead's mission abounded, not the least of which was the totally alien language of the natives. Yet in a mere six weeks the five-foot-two, 98-pound, 24-year-old anthropologist had absorbed so much of the language and customs that she could almost pass for a Samoan. After nine months of island life she returned to New York and wrote down her findings in a book titled *Coming of Age in Samoa*.

The book catapulted Mead to fame almost overnight. The most widely read work on anthropology ever, it struck a chord with American youth, especially in its descriptions of the casual sexual mores of the South Pacific and its declaration that Samoan adolescents did not suffer the angst so common in young Americans. She went on to study many other cultures, comparing their ways with Western ones and blending psychology with other disciplines, the better to illuminate the mysteries of human nature.

Later in life, as a professor at Columbia University, Mead, who kept her maiden name through three marriages, spoke widely and influentially on virtually any topic that struck her fancy. Some of her colleagues labeled her an "international busybody." One of them cracked, "Everybody talks about Margaret Mead, but nobody does anything about her." Furthermore, some of her most striking assertions about Samoan youth were proved inaccurate. Despite the sour grapes, Mead, who would eventually write 34 books and more than 1,300 articles, was a remarkable intellectual cross-pollinator whose rapport with the public was often envied but never equaled by less colorful academics.

Margaret Mead took six cotton dresses with her to Samoa but preferred dressing as a local, perhaps to encourage trust among the people she studied.

1926

Robert Goddard

America's Rocket Man

On a crisp March afternoon in 1926, Robert Goddard and his assistants crouched behind a metal barrier at his Aunt Effie's farm in Auburn, Massachusetts. Nearby stood a smoking 10-foot-tall contraption consisting of two fuel tanks, a rocket engine, and some interconnecting tubing, all held upright by a launch frame.

Goddard tripped a release mechanism, and after a pop, a blast of flame, and a roar, the device lifted off. "It looked almost magical as it rose," he wrote in his notes the next day. In two and a half seconds the missile climbed a majestic 41 feet, then crashed to earth in a nearby cabbage patch. Thus began and ended the modest career of the world's first liquid-fuel rocket, distant ancestor of the mighty Saturn V booster that four decades later would propel men to the moon.

Goddard had nursed a lifelong dream of space flight,

as described in Jules Verne's *A Voyage From the Earth to the Moon,* and in pursuit of that dream he studied physics, earning a doctorate in 1911 from Clark University, in Worcester, Massachusetts. In 1917 the Smithsonian Institution awarded him a $5,000 grant to do research on his idea of a solid-fuel rocket capable of reaching an altitude of several hundred miles. He soon abandoned solid fuels, however, for the greater power of gasoline and liquid oxygen.

Goddard pursued his research on rocketry as a physics professor at Clark (*above*). But needing more open land for his experiments than New England could offer, he moved to New Mexico. There, in 1930, he designed a rocket that soared to 2,000 feet and reached a velocity of 500 miles per hour.

Goddard continued to follow his dream, garnering 214 patents for rocketry-related inventions, including a multistage vehicle—without which space flight would still be just a theory. In 1962 NASA dedicated the Goddard Space Flight Center in Beltsville, Maryland, to the memory of America's pioneering rocket scientist.

Charles Lindbergh

The Lone Eagle

"Which way is Ireland?"

Charles Lindbergh, after countless hours aloft over the Atlantic, on circling down to hail a few small boats that signified the nearness of land

May 20, 1927, dawned damp and dreary at Long Island's Roosevelt Field, its clay runway softened by rain. On the strip stood a small plane bearing an immense load of fuel and the name *Spirit of St. Louis.* It was the vehicle that 25-year-old Charles Lindbergh would use in an attempt to be the first flier to cross the Atlantic solo. Lindbergh, in the cockpit, wondered whether the overloaded plane could even get off the ground. Attendants kicked out the wheel chocks, and he jammed the throttle forward. "Every cell of my being is on strike," he wrote about halfway through the seemingly endless flight. "It seems impossible to go on longer." But go on he did. A little more than 33 hours after takeoff he landed in Paris, welcomed by an overjoyed crowd of 100,000.

But triumph was displaced by horror for Lindbergh and his wife, Anne, in 1932. Their 20-month-old son, Charles Jr., was kidnapped and murdered, and after a highly publicized trial, an itinerant carpenter named Bruno Hauptmann was convicted of the crime and electrocuted. Sick of being hounded by the press, the Lindberghs moved to Europe. There, in the years leading up to World War II, Lindbergh tarnished his image by making pro-Nazi statements and campaigning for an isolationist American policy.

During the war he refurbished his reputation somewhat by serving as a consultant to the military at home and in the Pacific. Later the Lindberghs wrote several books, including Anne's *North to the Orient* and Charles's Pulitzer Prize-winning *Spirit of St. Louis,* that also helped soften the public's resentment.

The Babe, looking relatively trim early in his Yankee days, holds young fans spellbound behind the bleachers.

Babe Ruth

The Sultan of Swat

"Sixty, count 'em, 60," bellowed the New York Yankees' Babe Ruth of his 1927 home-run total. "Let some other son of a bitch match that!" His locker-room challenge would go unmet for more than 30 years.

George Herman Ruth was born February 6, 1895, in Baltimore, and spent most of his teen years in a reform school. At age 20 he signed with the minor-league Baltimore Orioles, where he picked up the nickname Babe. Ruth came to the big leagues with the Boston Red Sox as that rarest of rarities—a pitcher who could hit. A lefty, he won 24 games in 1917; in the 1918 World Series he pitched a record 29 ⅔ consecutive shutout innings. The next year the Sox made him a full-time outfielder, and he set another record—slamming 29 home runs. His power hitting skyrocketed after he was sold to the Yankees. He knocked 54 pitches over the wall in 1920, 59 in 1921. Then came the 60 of 1927.

Ruth was a crude, good-natured, womanizing hell-raiser who broke every training rule and got away with it. He was idolized by fans young and old, but he had a soft spot for kids. Once asked how he could justify making more than President Hoover, he replied, "I had a better year." He earned more than $2 million during his career—and spent most of it. "I lost $35,000 on one horse race alone," admitted the man who never outgrew the boy in him.

Virtuosos of the Long Ball

A fast-moving little pill, a war club, and the power in a slugger's arms combine for an instant, creating something thrilling. These players did it best.

Ted Williams
Though he lost five years to wartime service, Williams hit 521 lifetime homers.

Roger Maris
He broke Babe Ruth's season home-run record in his last game in 1961.

Mickey Mantle
Dogged by injuries, this switch-hitter still earned four slugging and home-run titles.

Willie Mays
With 660 home runs, Mays follows only Ruth and Aaron on the all-time list.

Reggie Jackson
The Yankees' "Mr. October" hit 563 homers—three in one Series game.

Mark McGwire
This huge Cardinal slammed out a record-smashing 70 home runs in 1998.

Sammy Sosa
Nose to nose with McGwire in 1998, he belted 66 for the Cubs by season's end.

Henry Aaron
Nobody did it better than the Braves' Hammerin' Hank, with a record 755 career home runs, as well as career marks for most games, at-bats, total bases, and RBIs—along with a .305 average for his 23 seasons.

1928

Alexander Fleming

Discoverer of Penicillin

As soon as you uncover a culture dish," bacteriologist Alexander Fleming once remarked, "something tiresome is sure to happen. Things fall out of the air." Sure enough, in the summer of 1928 a microscopic spore from a common mold, wafting in through a laboratory window, plunked down in a colony of bacteria under study by Fleming. Instead of being a nuisance, however, this particular speck of pollution would lead to one of the premier medical discoveries of all time: penicillin.

Fleming had left his Scottish farm home at age 13 to live with older brothers in London and seven years later started medical school, graduating in 1908. He had then toiled for 20 fruitless years in quest of a substance that could safely slow or stop infection in humans. That fateful summer Fleming was replicating the work of another scientist for an article on the often fatal bacterium staphylococcus. Picking up a dish of the pathogen in his cluttered lab, he noticed that it contained dewlike drops instead of the customary opaque yellow mass. Whatever had invaded the sample had killed the bacteria.

Analyzing the contents of the dish, he isolated the mold *Penicillium notatum* and cultivated it, extracting an elixir that proved lethal to a variety of bacteria. He called the substance penicillin, but more than a decade would pass before pathologist Howard Florey and chemist Ernst Chain succeeded in purifying it for use as a medicine—just in time to save countless soldiers' lives in World War II. Penicillin spurred the search for other antibiotics. Fleming, Florey, and Chain shared a Nobel Prize in 1945.

Makers of Medical Breakthroughs

During a century that saw more medical progress than in all previous history, some researchers made breakthroughs that stood out for their profound beneficial effects on the quality and length of human life. Here are a few of these inspired scientists.

Walter Reed *To prove that mosquitoes carry yellow fever, U.S. Army bacteriologist Reed led a team to Cuba in 1900. His findings permitted eradication of the illness in Havana by 1901.*

Jonas Salk *The world was freed from dread of the crippling and sometimes fatal polio in 1954 by Salk's injectable vaccine. Later, Albert Sabin developed an orally administered form.*

Frederick Banting *Losing a schoolmate to diabetes galvanized Banting to search for a cure. In 1921, investigating the pancreas, he isolated the life-giving hormone insulin.*

W. French Anderson *Gene therapy—repairing diseased cells by altering their genes—was born in 1990 when Anderson successfully treated a child with an immune-system disorder.*

Selman Waksman *Deaths from TB plummeted after Waksman introduced streptomycin in 1944. He coined the term "antibiotic" for substances that selectively attack microbes.*

David Ho *Not a cure for AIDS, but offering hope in the face of certain death, the antiviral drug "cocktail" therapy introduced by Ho in 1996 prolonged life for thousands of HIV patients.*

Willem Kolff *A pioneer in biomedical engineering, or bionics, Kolff developed the kidney dialysis machine as well as the heart-lung bypass machine, which makes open-heart surgery possible.*

Michael DeBakey *Famous for the artificial heart, DeBakey also made revolutionary advances in open-heart surgery, including the repair of aneurysms and blockages with Dacron tubing.*

1929

Edwin Hubble

Stargazer in an Expanding Universe

Scientists had long believed that the size of the universe was fixed. After the work of Edwin Hubble, they had to accept that it was expanding—and had been doing so for eons. In the late '20s another astronomer found that the stars appeared to be moving away from the earth. Seizing on this discovery, Hubble spent long hours at the telescope at the Mt. Wilson Observatory *(below)*, studying galaxies. In 1929 he asserted that the more distant a star or galaxy, the faster it is receding from earth—Hubble's law.

This finding, said cosmologist G. J. Whitrow, "made as great a change in man's conception of the universe as the Copernican revolution 400 years before," when Copernicus had disproved the theory that the earth was the center of the universe. Unaccountably, Nobel Prize committees overlooked Hubble's work, but he received many other tributes, and in 1990 NASA memorialized the great astronomer when it placed the Hubble Space Telescope in orbit.

1930

Sinclair Lewis

Scourge of American Complacency

During a single astounding decade Sinclair Lewis, shown above in 1937, published five bestselling novels, capping this run of creativity by winning the 1930 Nobel Prize for literature—the first American to do so. What distinguished these works was their satirical skewering of sacrosanct American institutions, from small towns to small (and big) business to the pulpit. *Main Street,* the first of the five, took a poke at provincialism in the fictional town of Gopher Prairie in Lewis's home state of Minnesota. The author went on to write of greed, hypocrisy, and closed-mindedness in *Babbitt, Arrowsmith, Elmer Gantry,* and *Dodsworth.*

Although Lewis's works written before and after this period passed virtually unnoticed, these five novels had a lasting impact on literature. "Without his writing," wrote Mark Schorer, Lewis's biographer, "one cannot imagine modern American literature. That is because, without his writing, we can hardly imagine ourselves."

Jane Addams

Fount of Human Kindness

When Jane Addams was awarded the Nobel Peace Prize in 1931, she was merely receiving due recognition for a lifetime spent promoting peace—and other blessings. Addams's peace quest had sprung largely from her experiences in founding Hull House in 1889 and operating this "settlement house" that aided the needy in one of Chicago's worst slums.

Addams observed that despite their poverty, the Greek, Italian, Russian, German, Irish, and other immigrants of the neighborhood enjoyed comparative social harmony. She formed a deep-seated belief that "the welfare of all nations is interdependent" and that political, intellectual, and religious tolerance was the cornerstone of world peace.

During World War I she headed the Woman's Peace Party, one of the first such movements in the U.S. As president of the International Congress of Women at The Hague, she lobbied for "continuous mediation" to end the war. After the armistice she helped found the Women's International League for Peace and Freedom, which she served as president for the rest of her life. Whatever time she had left over went to other progressive causes, such as the improvement of tenement and sweatshop conditions, an end to child labor, and woman suffrage.

"We have learned as common knowledge that much of the insensibility and hardness of the world is due to the lack of imagination which prevents a realization of the experience of other people."

Jane Addams, *Democracy and Social Ethics,* 1902

Some of the children whom philanthropist Jane Addams took under her wing visit their benefactor in 1930 during a 40th-anniversary celebration of the founding of Hull House.

Katharine Hepburn

Grace and Grit

When 25-year-old Katharine Hepburn made her 1932 film debut in *A Bill of Divorcement*, America discovered a new kind of feminine beauty. Lean and taut, she exuded an air of self-possessed independence. Offscreen she defined a new kind of glamour girl—an elegant, self-described "boy-woman."

Hepburn learned self-reliance early. Born into a progressive New England family, she grew up a tomboy who cropped her hair and called herself Jimmy. On Broadway and in Hollywood she retained an independent persona: "I . . . looked as if I was (and I *was*) hard to get. . . . never had any intention of getting married, wanted to paddle my own canoe." One critic wrote of her performance as the imperious Tracy Lord in 1940's *The Philadelphia Story (left)*: "When Katharine Hepburn sets out to play Katharine Hepburn, she is a sight to behold. Nobody is then her equal."

Hepburn's road to fame was not without obstacles. She struggled through a series of flop plays and movies in the mid-'30s, and one trade magazine dubbed her "box office poison." But she managed to carve out a career that spanned six decades, during which she racked up eight Academy Award nominations and four Oscars and gave the world a model for a new type of actress—one with grit as well as grace.

Golden Ladies of the Silver Screen

Whether sexy sirens, innocent ingénues, or serious artistes, these actresses became cultural icons, putting their indelible stamp on Hollywood.

Joan Crawford *One of Hollywood's most versatile female leads in the 1930s, Crawford refused to accept unglamorous roles as she aged, and she fell out of vogue. But she rallied to enormous success after age 38, starting with the Oscar-winning film Mildred Pierce in 1945.*

Bette Davis *"My eyes are basically my face," said Davis, whose huge peepers and exaggerated gestures made her unique. She portrayed powerful, independent women, earning Oscars for Dangerous (1935) and Jezebel (1938), as well as eight other nominations.*

Elizabeth Taylor *Defining '50s and '60s glamour with her voluptuous beauty, Taylor made more than 50 films, winning Oscars for Butterfield 8 (1960) and Who's Afraid of Virginia Woolf (1966). But her personal life was fraught with tragedy, excess, and scandal.*

Audrey Hepburn *A childhood survivor of Nazi-occupied Holland, Hepburn at 24 brought a fresh, delicate beauty to her first U.S. film, Roman Holiday (1953), which netted her an Oscar. She affirmed her stardom with the blockbuster Sabrina (1954).*

Meryl Streep *Starting out in the '70s, Streep sought complex roles that showcased her emotional range and—as in Sophie's Choice (1982) and Out of Africa (1985)—her talent for accents. She considered acting a serious craft but claimed no particular method.*

Kept in dresses and long hair by his doting mother until age six, Franklin graduated to sailor suits.

FDR, scion of a society family, poses (front row, center) with football teammates at Groton School.

As assistant navy secretary, Roosevelt enjoys an outing with Eleanor (right) and friends.

1932

Franklin D. Roosevelt
An Aristocrat for the Common Man

When Americans went to the polls in 1932 to elect a president, the nation was in the throes of catastrophe. One quarter of all workers had lost their jobs in the economic collapse of the Great Depression. Despairing voters gave a landslide victory to Democrat Franklin Delano Roosevelt, choosing a man in a wheelchair to get the country back on its feet.

In his inaugural address FDR told a cheering crowd, "The only thing we have to fear is fear itself." The Harvard-educated aristocrat, shown at right in a typical upbeat pose, knew well the truth of those words. An attack of polio at age 39 had crippled his legs but done little to slow his robust political career, which had begun in 1911 with his election to the New York State Senate. President Wilson picked him to be assistant secretary of the navy in 1913. He later was elected governor of New York State. Now he was president, and his easy smile and unwavering optimism pumped confidence into a demoralized and fearful citizenry.

Roosevelt's first action in the White House was to rescue the nation's banks, which were failing left and right. Declaring a bank holiday, he summoned Congress to a special session to pass the Emergency Banking Act. Then he went on the radio with the first of his "fireside chats," explaining calmly and honestly to the nation how the system worked. When banks later reopened with no long lines of panicked customers, one of Roosevelt's advisers remarked, "Capitalism was saved in eight days."

In the first 100 days of his administration, Roosevelt bulldozed through the Congress 15 pieces of revolutionary legislation to bring about about economic recovery. Many features of the New Deal, as his program was called, endure as a legacy—Social Security, the Federal Deposit Insurance Corporation, the Securities and Exchange Commission, and the minimum wage. Other New Deal programs served their purpose and expired; some were eventually ruled unconstitutional or simply didn't work.

In the middle of Roosevelt's second term, signs of bad things to come appeared when Hitler annexed Austria and Japan invaded China. With war looming, voters elected FDR to an unprecedented third term in 1940; they kept him in office as war leader in 1944. But his health was failing, and he died on April 12, 1945, a few weeks before Germany surrendered.

A frail FDR poses with Winston Churchill, Joseph Stalin, and aides in February 1945 at the Yalta Conference.

Adolf Hitler

Ideologue of Hatred and Horror

In a period of just eight years beginning in 1933, Adolf Hitler spread his malignant dominion over most of Europe and North Africa. His spectacular rise grew out of dismal political and economic conditions in Europe, acted upon by his warped, driven personality.

Born in Austria in 1889, young Adolf *(inset)* was spoiled by his mother and bullied by his father, a civil servant. A classmate recalled the boy as a stiff and remote loner. As a young man he was grandiose, brooding, and inflamed with a hatred of Jews. He served with bravery, however, in the German army during the Great War.

Working for the army as a political spy in the ideological and economic chaos of postwar Germany, Hitler infiltrated the tiny, rabidly nationalist German Workers' Party. He quickly fell in with its program and by 1921 had taken control of the group, now called the National Socialist German Workers' (Nazi) Party.

An awkward orator, Hitler practiced emphatic gestures to bring forcefulness and emotional impact to his speeches *(right)*. His voice, said one follower, was like a knife that opened each raw wound, "liberating the mass unconscious, expressing its innermost aspirations, telling it what it most wants to hear." Largely on the strength of his hypnotic public harangues, his party grew by the early '30s into one of the most powerful in Germany.

In 1933 Hitler was named chancellor, and he soon cast aside legal restraints to institute a brutal dictatorship. He ended the country's economic doldrums by putting it on a war footing, and in speech after speech he incited the populace to fanatical nationalism. After annexing Austria in 1937 and eliminating Czechoslovakia by degrees in 1938 and '39, he attacked Poland on September 1, 1939, touching off World War II. Concurrently he initiated plans that would culminate in the murder of six million Jews and millions of other "subhumans." But by 1944 Germany itself was under siege from the Allies. In early 1945, as his Third Reich collapsed around him, he withdrew to his Führerbunker, deep beneath the bombed-out center of Berlin, and on April 30 he shot himself.

Scores of thousands of worshipful Germans assemble in Bückeberg in 1934 to place themselves under the Führer's diabolical spell.

Notable 20th-Century Tyrants

Like Hitler, the men shown here instigated brutal executions, secret murders, and mass killings to hold whole populations in thrall.

Kim Il-sung *Ruler of Communist North Korea, Kim started a bloody war in 1950, then executed thousands of dissidents and sealed his country's borders, banning outside contact during his 46-year reign.*

Idi Amin Dada *Amin, dictator of Uganda during the 1970s, used the thugs of his "State Research Bureau" to murder an estimated 300,000 people. He kept the severed heads of prominent victims in a freezer in his house.*

Pol Pot *Communist head of Cambodia's genocidal Khmer Rouge regime in the late 1970s, Pol Pot oversaw the slaughter of anywhere between 1 and 3 million of the country's 8 million people.*

Saddam Hussein *Taking over Iraq in 1979, Hussein attacked Iran in a war that killed 1.5 million and then used poison gas on the Kurds. Perhaps 100,000 of his own soldiers died in the 1991 Gulf War.*

1934

George Balanchine

Master of Balletic Choreography

"This will be the most important letter I will ever write you," began Lincoln Kirstein, a wealthy American art patron, in a breathless note to a friend in 1933. "My pen burns my hand as I write." Kirstein's news was that he had persuaded famed Russian-born choreographer George Balanchine *(above)* to help bring professional ballet to the States.

Balanchine had begun his career with a rush when, in 1924, at age 20, he was named ballet master for Diaghilev's Ballets Russes in Paris. In 1934 he founded the School of American Ballet; there, and at the New York City Ballet, which he and Kirstein created in 1948, Balanchine abandoned many conventions of classical ballet and introduced abstract dance. He choreographed expressly for American dancers and established the long-necked, impossibly thin look as the norm for ballerinas.

1935

Martha Graham

Empress of Avant-Garde Dance

She was not the first to move beyond classical ballet—Isadora Duncan and Ruth St. Denis had preceded her—but Martha Graham crystallized modern dance as a new art form and was among the first native-born celebrities of the American avant-garde. In 1935, collaborating with Japanese sculptor Isamu Noguchi, she produced *Frontier*, whose bizarre-looking set caused an uproar. No rococo ballroom or painted landscape for Graham. Noguchi tied two ropes at an angle to a bench and voilà! The American prairie.

Graham's inspiration for the set was a childhood vision. Born in Pennsylvania in 1894, she had moved with her family to California at the age of 14. The train that carried them across the broad American West ran on tracks that became for her "parallel lines whose meaning was inexhaustible, whose purpose was infinite." Her father viewed dance as unsuitable for a young lady, and not until he died was she able to pursue her muse. She began her training at the unheard-of advanced age of 22 with Ted Shawn and Ruth St. Denis's Denishawn troupe in Los Angeles. The exotic repertoire there drew heavily on foreign cultures and mythic forms and was well suited to Graham, whose physical features and free movement impressed Shawn as "tigerish . . . primitive . . . passionate and regal."

In the late 1920s she founded her own company, the Dance Repertory Theater, whose signature was the abstract, expressive gesture. Unlike all other familiar forms of entertainment, hers was delivered without elaborate props and sets, pared to the barest architecture of movement. Not everyone got it. Graham was second only to Eleanor Roosevelt as the most caricatured figure of the '30s. *Time* magazine referred to *Frontier* as "High Priestess Martha Graham and her surrealist fence act." Danny Kaye satirized her in a musical revue with a chorus line called *Graham Crackers*, and the classical choreographer Michel Fokine summarized a Graham piece as "ugly girl makes ugly movements on stage while ugly mother tells ugly brother to make ugly sounds on drum." Graham was unfazed—she *meant* to be provocative. With bare feet, striking makeup, and ebony hair stretched tightly off what one critic called her "Easter Island mask of a face," she choreographed and danced well into old age. When once asked how long she intended to continue, she replied, "As long as I've got an audience."

The fabric of her gown emphasizes her body architecture as Martha Graham dances: the crook of the elbow, the angle of the hand, the arm extended.

1936

Eleanor Roosevelt
A New Kind of First Lady

"It isn't enough to talk about peace. One must believe in it. And it isn't enough to believe in it. One must work at it."

Eleanor Roosevelt, 1951

Roasting hot dogs over a picnic fire for the king and queen of England or descending into a coal mine to talk to the miners, Eleanor Roosevelt changed the role of first lady. She was the first to hold press conferences, the first to do away with stiff formality in the White House, and the first to mix freely with the public.

In 1936 she set yet another precedent by starting a syndicated daily newspaper column, "My Day," in which she chatted about White House family doings and offered advice: "The things you refuse to meet today always come back at you later on, usually under circumstances which make the decision twice as difficult as it originally was." The column was also a sounding board for her often controversial political views.

Eleanor had not always been so bold. Born in 1884 into New York's prominent Roosevelt family—Theodore *(pages 16-17)* was her uncle—she was a shy, serious child. Her mother, beautiful and vain, told her that she was hopelessly ugly and ridiculed her in public. Following such episodes, Eleanor recalled, "I wanted to sink through the floor in shame." With the support of teachers and friends, however, she began to blossom. "More and more I used the quickness of my mind to pick the minds of other people and use their knowledge as my own." Eleanor's intellect and social conscience attracted her distant cousin Franklin Delano Roosevelt *(pages 70-72)*, and they married in 1905. Still, it was only when she entered the White House in 1933, after 28 years of marriage and six children, that she developed into the confident public figure whose concern for the oppressed and downtrodden won the nation's heart.

During her 12-plus years as first lady, Eleanor—to the fury of conservatives—championed such causes as women's rights and equal opportunities for black Americans. As Claire Booth Luce put it, "No woman has ever so comforted the distressed or so distressed the comfortable." Even after FDR's death she remained active, serving as a delegate to the United Nations, lecturing, and writing. When she died at 78 in 1962, *Time* magazine proclaimed her "the world's most admired and talked-about woman."

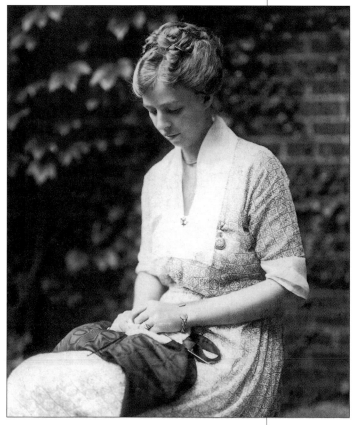

Eleanor Roosevelt at 35 (above) seemed shy and fragile. A year earlier she had learned that FDR was having an affair with her social secretary. At 60 (opposite), she appeared confident and strong.

1937

Walt Disney
Master of Fantasy

Cinderella Castle looms over the "cast members" assembled in 1971 to run Florida's Walt Disney World Resort. Disney planned this second of his vast theme parks but died five years before its opening.

> "The short subject was just a filler on any program. I felt I just had to diversify my business. Now, if I could crack the feature field, then I could do things."

Walt Disney, on the making of
Snow White and the Seven Dwarfs

When the creator of cartoon hero Mickey Mouse *(inset, below)* unveiled his idea for a full-length animated film, Hollywood skeptics warned Walt Disney that he was overreaching. But *Snow White and the Seven Dwarfs,* an 83-minute cartoon that premiered in 1937, was a smash hit. Indeed, the movie became so firmly embedded in the minds of those who saw it that for the rest of their lives any thought of Snow White conjured up only images of Disney's colorful, bouncy characters, not the dour Germanic figures of the Brothers Grimm tale.

Making this first-ever feature-length opus from some two million colored drawings took four years and $1.5 million and almost bankrupted Disney's young company. But the risk proved well worth it. The movie generated a deluge of income that continues to pour in even today.

The man who reaped the rewards of this gold mine had first seized the imaginations of audiences in 1928 in a black-and-white music-filled cartoon short called *Steamboat Willie.* There the world met that irrepressibly jaunty personality Mickey Mouse, who proved so popular that the studio began producing his cartoons monthly. Disney added other characters to what became a pantheon of cartoon archetypes, including the irascible Donald Duck and the hapless yet amiable Goofy. Audiences were enthralled.

After *Snow White and the Seven Dwarfs* came a hit parade of other full-length animated features, including *Pinocchio, Fantasia, Dumbo, Bambi, Sleeping Beauty,* and *Cinderella.* Beginning in 1954 Disney also became a fixture in American living rooms with a TV series that would run, under *Disneyland* and other titles, for 29 consecutive years, scoring perhaps its greatest success with its five-part Davy Crockett miniseries. A weekday-afternoon kids' feature, *The Mickey Mouse Club,* became an American cultural institution during a four-year run starting in 1955.

A friend once called Walt Disney a "visionary handyman who has built a whole industry out of daydreams." Disney gave his daydreams physical form in 1955 with Disneyland, the first of a series of truly phenomenal "theme" amusement parks. Before he died in 1966 his films had won 42 Oscars, and his lively imagination had earned him a place in history as the century's preeminent master of fantasy.

A silhouetted Mickey Mouse presents his boss, the nattily attired Walt Disney, in the mid-1930s.

Orson Welles

The Boy Wonder

The term "boy wonder" could have been invented for Orson Welles. He was only 23 when he unintentionally scared Americans out of their wits on Halloween Night 1938 with a radio production of H. G. Wells's 1898 sci-fi classic, *The War of the Worlds*. The show's use of realistic news bulletins to chronicle a Martian invasion was so convincing that many terrified New Jerseyites headed for the hills and others cowered in their cellars for days. At an even younger age he had stunned New York theater audiences with an all-black, voodoo-flavored *Macbeth* and an audacious modern-dress *Julius Caesar*, with actors uniformed as Italian Fascists.

Most impressively, Welles was only 25 when he conceived, co-wrote, produced, directed, and starred in his first feature film, *Citizen Kane*—a thinly disguised take on the life of press lord William Randolph Hearst and widely held to be the greatest movie ever made. Welles himself played Charles Foster Kane, the Hearstlike character *(inset)*. He enlisted a brilliant screenwriter to coauthor the script and an imaginative cameraman to shoot the production. The result was a movie that delivered its powerful emotions, ingenious plot, and masterful performances through revolutionary film techniques. Critics praised it; other directors adopted its cinematic innovations; and people have never stopped talking about it since it was released in 1941. But thanks to a Hearst-backed campaign to keep it out of theaters, it did not earn much money.

Welles made more brilliant movies that were commercial failures—from *The Magnificent Ambersons* (1942) to *Touch of Evil*, in 1958. By now he was being called "the aging boy wonder." "The word 'genius' was whispered into my ear . . . while I was mewling in my crib," Welles told a biographer, "so it never occurred to me that I wasn't [one] until middle age."

Critics overwhelmingly agree he *was* a genius, but one whose creative powers peaked early. Some contend he had an unconscious desire to fail; others, that his towering talent was defeated by moneygrubbing studio executives. Still, as critic Richard Corliss reminded readers upon Welles's death in 1985, "The man did make movies."

Before his rich, urgent baritone terrified listeners in War of the Worlds, Welles had already won fame as the voice of "The Shadow" in a popular radio show of that name. The show's tag line, delivered in sepulchral tones, became a catch phrase: "Who knows what evil lurks in the hearts of men? The Shadow knows."

Frank Sinatra

Chairman of the Board

Eyes bright and hair neatly brushed, Francis Albert Sinatra, born in 1915 in Hoboken, New Jersey, sits for his First Communion portrait.

Adoring girls mob Sinatra after a 1943 show. In 1944 30,000 bobbysoxers, unable to get into his sold-out concert, rioted in Times Square.

He's never had a hit record," said bemused bandleader Harry James in 1939 of a singer he was thinking of signing. "He looks like a wet rag. But he says he's the greatest! His name is Sinatra." At age 23 Frank Sinatra overflowed with confidence. After cutting a string of hits with James and then with Tommy Dorsey's band, he made his first solo appearance at New York's Paramount Theater on December 30, 1942. The event produced a new phenomenon: thousands of female fans screaming, crying, even fainting. Newspapers dubbed him Swoonatra, and contracts for radio, records, movies, and personal appearances poured in.

Sinatra refined his art. He studied the styles of Bing Crosby and Billie Holiday. He learned to plot every gesture and still make it appear casual. By watching Dorsey, who could play eight bars on a trumpet on one breath, he mastered breath control. This skill enabled him to croon long passages conveying single thoughts, one reason his songs seem intimate and personal.

"I did it my way."

Frank Sinatra

Sinatra's popularity slumped in the late '40s, but an Oscar-winning performance in the 1953 film *From Here to Eternity* revived his career. He became the swingin' Sinatra, Chairman of the Board, leader of the Rat Pack, a notorious womanizer who partied nonstop with show-biz pals, politicians, and the occasional mob figure while putting out a dazzling series of top-selling albums.

Though he made fewer and fewer records and films through the 1970s, he tirelessly continued to give concerts. Even on his last tour in the late 1980s with Rat Pack buddies Dean Martin and Sammy Davis Jr., Sinatra remained a nocturnal animal, insisting on partying till dawn. "You've got to love livin', baby!" he said. "Because dyin' is a pain in the ass!"

Sinatra packs his sexy charm into a song at New York's Riobamba nightclub in 1943, a gig that proved his magic worked on grownups as well as teenagers.

1940

Winston Churchill
Unyielding Guardian at the Gates of Freedom

Resplendent in his Fourth Hussars uniform, Second Lieutenant Winston Churchill ponders his future on graduating from Sandhurst in 1895. He came under gunfire that year, on his 21st birthday.

Churchill strides through a bombed-out London street in 1940 on one of his frequent inspections. Crowds often cheered the 65-year-old prime minister and urged him to "give it 'em back."

I have nothing to offer you," said Britain's new prime minister in May 1940, "but blood, toil, tears and sweat"—a hard truth as only Winston Churchill, shown at right in a famous contemporary portrait, could deliver it. At that moment Nazi Germany was overrunning western Europe and beginning to eye Britain. Churchill would be charged with the defense not only of his country but of the rest of the free world.

He seemed destined for the role. Born into a noble family in 1874, he distinguished himself in the Boer War as both a soldier and a correspondent, was elected to Parliament in 1900, and took a cabinet seat in 1908. He experienced sharp ups and downs during World War I and the interwar period but earned renown from a series of eloquently written histories. Now, at Britain's lowest ebb, Churchill was in residence at No. 10 Downing Street. He defied Hitler implacably, striving to forge a strong alliance against the Nazis by wooing American support and, after the Germans attacked the Soviet Union, even making common cause with his longtime foe Stalin.

Nothing was more symbolic of his wartime leadership than his stirring speeches. In tribute to the young fighter pilots of the RAF he declared, "Never in the field of human conflict has so much been owed by so many to so few." By the time Hitler was finally destroyed, it could be said that the same gratitude was owed by all freedom-loving peoples to Churchill and his small island nation.

As the anti-Nazi alliance fell apart after the war, Churchill performed another service for democracy when he warned of Stalin's imprisonment of eastern Europe, stating, "An iron curtain has descended across the Continent." For the war-weary West his analysis, however unwelcome, proved as accurate as his earlier perception of Adolf Hitler.

1941

Charles Drew
Father of the Blood Bank

With the outbreak of World War II, Britain was desperately short of blood to treat its escalating number of casualties, and it appealed for help to a most unlikely figure—given the social climate of the time. Dr. Charles Drew (*above*), a young black professor of medicine at Howard University, had carried out groundbreaking research demonstrating that plasma—blood fluid from which the cells and platelets have been removed—was safer and more convenient to store and distribute than whole blood. Drew set up and operated a system for collecting and processing plasma for America's ally.

As war loomed for the United States, the American Red Cross in 1941 tapped Drew to organize its blood bank. But racism caught up with him: Military officials barred black blood donors. He resigned in protest and returned to educating young black medical students at Howard.

1942

J. Robert Oppenheimer
Ambivalent Builder of the Atomic Bomb

When J. Robert Oppenheimer, a 38-year-old professor of nuclear physics, was asked in 1942 to head up the U.S. government's ultrasecret effort to develop an atomic bomb—code-named the Manhattan Project—he gladly accepted the challenge and was soon setting up a heavily guarded laboratory complex in remote Los Alamos, New Mexico. Yet after three years of grueling work, when his moment of triumph arrived and he watched the first test bomb explode in 1945, an ominous couplet from the Hindu Bhagavad-Gita flashed through Oppenheimer's mind: "I am become Death, the destroyer of worlds."

A man of encyclopedic learning from a cultured German Jewish family in New York City, Oppenheimer had read those lines in the original San-

---

"The physicists have known sin; and this is a knowledge which they cannot lose."

J. Robert Oppenheimer, in a 1947 speech to fellow physicists

---

skrit; it was just one of the eight languages he knew. He also had a genius for administration, working with army general Leslie Groves to keep the 4,500 workers at Los Alamos moving toward their goal at an amazing clip.

Ultimately, Oppenheimer's accomplishments at Los Alamos came into conflict with his conscience. Although the atomic bombs dropped on Hiroshima and Nagasaki in August 1945 forced Japan to surrender and brought World War II to an unexpectedly early end, he was profoundly troubled by the death, devastation, and residual suffering the bombs caused, and he soon left Los Alamos to return to teaching. From then on, he was a determined opponent of the proliferation of the very weapons whose creation he had masterminded. His opinions, and his forceful arguments, uttered during a period of national hysteria over the perceived menace of domestic Communism, won him many enemies, and in 1954 he was stripped of his security clearance because of alleged "defects of character." It was the price paid by a physicist who could not deny his better nature.

Jacques Cousteau

Trailblazer of the Briny Deep

Jacques Cousteau had an obsession: to swim underwater like a fish, unencumbered by an airhose or cable running to the surface. In 1936, as an officer in the French navy, he was given a pair of pearl-diver's goggles and was astonished by what he could see—"wildlife, untouched, a jungle at the border of the sea, never seen by those who floated on the opaque roof."

Inspired, he collaborated with an engineer to develop a device that he called the aqualung. It consisted of air tanks and a pressure regulator that, strapped to the diver's back, delivered air at the pressure of the surrounding depths, permitting safe and easy breathing. With this invention, introduced in 1943, Cousteau *(right)* was launched on a lifetime of exploring beneath the seas and sharing his discoveries with the world through TV documentaries. It also allowed recreational swimmers to dive and, as he said, to be "born into another world."

This 1958 photo captures what admirers called Oppenheimer's "genius look." At the time he was director of Princeton's Institute for Advanced Study.

The first nuclear test bomb, nicknamed Fat Man, explodes in the New Mexico desert on July 16, 1945, with a flash of light seen in three states.

Young Dwight Eisenhower (center, front) is shown with friends on a camping trip in 1907.

Eisenhower and his wife, Mamie, hold their son Doud, who died of scarlet fever at age three.

Ike addresses members of the First Infantry Division in France four weeks after D-Day.

1944

Dwight D. Eisenhower
Guiding Hand of the D-Day Invasion

When the vast Anglo-American amphibious force swarmed onto the beaches of Normandy, France, on D-Day, June 6, 1944, it was acting on the orders of a single man, Allied supreme commander Dwight David Eisenhower. The 53-year-old general, known to everyone simply as Ike, had made what he later called "the most agonizing decision of my life"—to launch, despite extremely risky weather conditions, the cross-Channel attack that would be the beginning of the end for Adolf Hitler.

A soldier who hated war, a hero who never courted heroism—ultimately, a politician who abhorred politics—Ike *(right, in 1946)* was well prepared for the momentous responsibilities he would bear that day. Born on October 14, 1890, in Denison, Texas, he was raised mainly in Abilene, Kansas, by Mennonite parents who imbued their sons with the pioneer creed of individualism and hard work. After graduating from West Point in 1915, he organized the army's first tank unit during World War I and then slowly rose in the peacetime army, becoming an aide to army chief of staff Douglas MacArthur in 1933. In June 1941 Ike was made chief of staff, Third Army, and he received his first star three months later.

By the time Roosevelt picked Ike to command the assault on Normandy, he was a four-star general and had led successful invasions of French North Africa, Sicily, and Italy. He was known for a down-to-earth manner, resolute idealism, and organizational genius, but what sealed Roosevelt's decision were Ike's first-rate political talents, which had served him well in holding together the sometimes touchy British-American partnership.

In the postwar years he was a prize that both major parties wooed as a presidential candidate. The Republicans won out, and in 1952 "I Like Ike" fervor swept him into office for the first of two terms. In the White House the man of war gave his country peace. He fulfilled his pledge to end the Korean War, reduced the size of the armed forces, and refused to jump into an arms race with the Soviet Union. Yet memories of his World War II performance remained strong. When he died in 1969, a mourning Frenchman left this message at the American embassy in Paris. "To General Eisenhower, in deep homage also to those who fell on the beaches of Normandy. We shall never forget."

Top U.S. Military Leaders of World War II

Although America's armed forces had just been through a 20-year period of stagnation when the war came, this remarkable group of officers emerged to answer the nation's need for outstanding generalship. All but Curtis LeMay had served in World War I.

General Omar Bradley *Having been Ike's field representative in the North African campaign, Bradley went on to command the 12th Army Group, which liberated much of western Europe in 1945.*

General George S. Patton *The tough, flamboyant Patton drove his Third Army across France in 1944, hopped the Rhine in 1945, and smashed through the heart of Germany to Czechoslovakia.*

General Carl Spaatz *"Tooey" Spaatz orchestrated a massive daylight bombing campaign from England supported by long-range fighter escorts that soundly defeated the Luftwaffe by D-Day.*

General Douglas MacArthur *Driven from the Philippines in 1942, MacArthur fulfilled a vow to return as he led a brilliant campaign to bring American forces within striking distance of Japan.*

Admiral Chester Nimitz *As Pacific commander, Nimitz restored the navy's confidence after Pearl Harbor, launching a carrier-based ambush at Midway in 1942 that doomed the Japanese navy.*

Lieutenant General Holland M. Smith *Leader of bloody marine assaults on Tarawa, Saipan, and Iwo Jima, "Howlin' Mad" Smith was, at 62, America's oldest fighting three-star general.*

Major General Curtis E. LeMay *An innovative air tactician, LeMay sent his B-29 Superfortresses on low-level incendiary raids in 1945 that destroyed 25 percent of Tokyo in a firestorm.*

Top Allied and Axis Combat Commanders of World War II

*Like their American counterparts, the Allied and Axis command-
ers below were well trained and intelligent and possessed those*
*qualities of courage, self-confidence, ferocity, and authority that
made their word law and their command decisions effective.*

General Charles de Gaulle
*When France fell in 1940, de Gaulle
refused to capitulate, instead creating the Free French movement
in London and leading it until
la Patrie was liberated in 1944.*

**General Field Marshal
Erwin Rommel** *One of
Hitler's most charismatic
generals, Rommel conquered
much of North Africa in
1942. He later built the
Atlantic Wall and led the
defenders at Normandy.*

**General Bernard Law
Montgomery** *As com-
mander of the British Eighth
Army in North Africa,
"Monty" routed Rommel's
forces at El Alamein in 1942.
Later he led the Allied
ground forces at Normandy.*

**Admiral Isoroku
Yamamoto** *Planner of
the devastating attack on
Pearl Harbor, Yamamoto
later was trumped at
Midway. He was killed
in 1943 when his plane
was ambushed by U.S.
fighter planes.*

**Admiral Lord Louis
Mountbatten** *Mountbatten,
a great-grandson of Queen
Victoria, led his Southeast Asia
command in the reconquest of
Burma and accepted the Japanese surrender at Singapore.*

Marshal Georgy Zhukov
*Considered the Red Army's best
field commander, Zhukov
stopped the Germans at the
gates of Moscow in the desper-
ate days of 1941 and captured
Berlin in 1945.*

**General Field Marshal Erich von
Manstein** *The mastermind behind the
German Blitzkrieg against France in 1940,
von Manstein went on to fight in Russia
but was fired by Hitler for advocating tac-
tical retreats.*

1945

Harry S Truman

The Man From Missouri

One night during the 1944 election campaign, Democratic vice-presidential candidate Harry Truman had a nightmare: President Roosevelt had died, and the immense responsibility of leading a nation at war fell to him. On April 12, 1945, Truman's nightmare came true. A senator from Missouri since 1935, Truman had only reluctantly accepted the vice-presidential nomination. Now, he anxiously faced the burdens of the presidency. The day after he was sworn in Truman appealed to a group of reporters: "Boys, if you ever pray, pray for me now. I don't know whether you fellows ever had a load of hay fall on you, but when they told me yesterday what had happened, I felt like the moon, the stars, and all the planets had fallen on me."

Truman passed his youth *(inset, at age 10)* in Independence, a farm town near Kansas City, and grew up plain-spoken, honest, and unpretentious. After serving in France in World War I as an artillery officer, he won election in 1922, at age 38, as county judge—the title used in Missouri for county commissioner. From then on, politics was his business.

As president, he made difficult decisions without flinching. He ordered atomic bombs to be used against Japan. Opposing postwar isolationist sentiments, he announced the Truman Doctrine, which pledged the United States to help countries threatened by Communism, and he initiated the Marshall Plan to provide massive economic aid to war-ravaged Europe. At home he backed civil rights and ordered racial integration of the armed forces. In the 1948 election, with most of the press rabidly against him and the polls counting him out, Truman beat Republican Thomas Dewey in a stupendous upset, winning four years of the presidency in his own right.

In 1950 he committed troops to South Korea to save that country from being overrun by Communist forces. The following year Truman—never one to suffer insults to himself, the presidency, or the Constitution—fired the immensely popular General Douglas MacArthur for insubordination. Little respected when he first took office, Truman would be judged by history as one of the nation's great presidents.

Lauren Bacall plays torch singer to Vice President Truman's accompaniment at a servicemen's party in 1945. In his teens Truman practiced two hours a day.

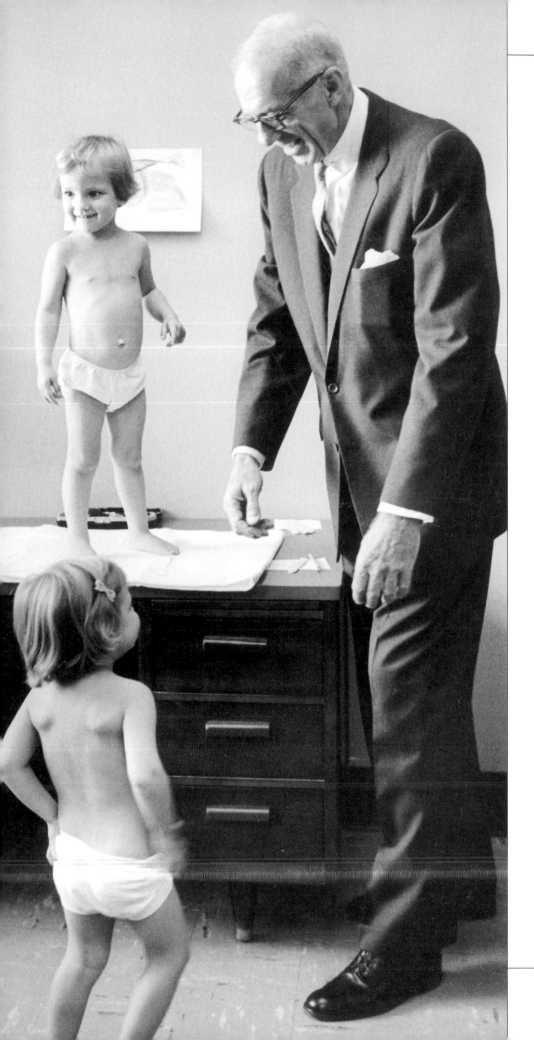

Benjamin Spock

Baby Doctor to a Nation

In 1946, just as the baby boom was starting, a 43-year-old pediatrician named Benjamin Spock published *The Common Sense Book of Baby and Child Care.* Dr. Spock's advice was remarkably different from the authoritarian prescriptions found in other books. Dr. John B. Watson's longtime standard, *Psychological Care of Infant and Child,* for example, said, "Never, never kiss your child." Spock disagreed: "Don't be afraid to kiss your baby when you feel like it." He assured parents that feeding babies when they were hungry instead of on a strict schedule would do no harm, nor would picking up a crying baby. Trained in psychiatry and psychoanalysis, Spock, shown here in 1962, was convinced that a more relaxed, flexible approach was good for the emotional health of both parent and child, though he counseled his readers that firm, loving discipline was also essential.

In the '60s critics accused him of promoting "permissiveness" and blamed him for the rebelliousness of a generation of youth raised on his advice. His stock declined further when he opposed nuclear weapons testing, the Vietnam War, and the draft. Sales of *Baby and Child Care* slumped during this period, but eventually picked up again. By the time of his death in 1998, the book had sold nearly 50 million copies in 42 languages—second only to the Bible.

J. Presper Eckert and John W. Mauchly

Unwitting Founders of a Social Revolution

During World War II a computing laboratory at the University of Pennsylvania was producing artillery ballistics tables for the army, using slow, mechanical calculators. Two staff members, electrical engineering graduate student J. Presper Eckert *(below, left)* and physicist John W. Mauchly *(right)*, agreed that the lab needed a digital machine—one that computed electronically, not mechanically. Although constructing one would be expensive, and Eckert and Mauchly couldn't guarantee the results, the army gave them a go-ahead in April 1943.

Eckert, just 24, was an engineering wizard who had built a crystal radio set on a pencil when he was eight; Mauchly, 35, understood the mathematics and physics of trajectories. It took them two and a half years to build their machine, but it was worth the wait. Unveiled on February 16, 1946, the world's first electronic digital computer, ENIAC (short for Electrical Numerical Integrator and Computer), was 1,000 times faster than the best mechanical calculator. A technological—and ultimately a social—revolution had been launched.

George C. Marshall

The Author of Europe's Postwar Recovery

He entered the army in 1902 as a second lieutenant; 37 years later, with World War II looming, he became chief of staff. A man of towering intellect and character, General George Catlett Marshall oversaw a massive buildup of America's armed forces and guided them through the war.

In 1947 Marshall became secretary of state *(right, with a Cub Scout),* and in that role he made a grim assessment of war-torn Europe's condition. "The patient is sinking," he said, "while the doctors deliberate." The region's economy was in chaos, its people were demoralized, and the Communist Party was rapidly gaining strength in countries where it had enjoyed scant appeal before the war.

Speaking at Harvard University's June 1947 commencement, Marshall announced an end to deliberation. With his impassive face and understated speaking style, he outlined a historic proposal so quietly that it barely caused a stir in his audience: that America commit itself to an economic recovery program for Europe.

Congress approved $17 billion for the Marshall Plan, and Europe, as British foreign minister Ernest Bevin said, "grabbed the life line with both hands." Before the aid program ended in 1952, it was so successful that most sectors of European industry had far exceeded their prewar output. In 1953 Marshall—"a superman," according to an admiring subordinate—was awarded the Nobel Peace Prize.

1947

Jackie Robinson

Crossing Baseball's "Color Line"

The 28-year-old rookie infielder who stepped up to the plate for the Brooklyn Dodgers at Ebbets Field on the cold, rainy afternoon of April 15, 1947, was not merely taking his first turn at bat: John Roosevelt "Jackie" Robinson was stepping up to the plate of history to knock Jim Crow out of baseball. That walk to the plate had begun back in 1945, when general manager Branch Rickey signed the former college four-letter athlete *(inset)* to play with the Dodgers' Montreal Royals farm team. At their first meeting Rickey kept underscoring the taunts, indignities, and ha-

tred the first black player in organized baseball would face. Robinson asked, "Mr. Rickey, do you want a ballplayer who's afraid to fight back?" Rickey replied, "I want a player with guts enough *not* to fight back."

Robinson came close to cracking many times. "For one wild and rage-crazed minute," he later wrote of a 1947 game when the Philadelphia Phillies and their manager bombarded him with racial obscenities, "I thought, to hell with Mr. Rickey's 'noble experiment.' " But Robinson controlled himself and fought back only on the playing field, where he batted .297 for the year with 125 runs scored and a team-leading 29 stolen bases. Weathering abuse that ranged from bean balls to death threats, he ended the season as major-league baseball's first-ever Rookie of the Year.

Before he retired 10 years later, Robinson would win the National League batting title and Most Valuable Player award in 1949, lead the Dodgers to six pennants and a world championship, and record a career batting average of .311. By the time he died from a heart attack in 1972, African American superstars were common in both major leagues, ample testament to the gains his courage and determination had won. As sportswriter Red Smith put it, "The word for Jackie Robinson is 'unconquerable.' . . . He would not be defeated. Not by the other team and not by life."

Jackie Robinson displays his aggressive base-running style in a daring attempt to steal home in a 1949 game against catcher Rube Walker and the Chicago Cubs.

1947

Chuck Yeager

Exemplar of "The Right Stuff"

One night U.S. Air Force test pilot Chuck Yeager and his wife, Glennis, went on a horseback ride. Yeager's horse hit a fence in the dark and he was thrown, breaking some ribs. He told no one about the accident, because in a few days, on October 14, 1947, he was due to try to break something else: the sound barrier.

Nobody found out about the mishap, and Yeager got his chance. Moments after dropping free from the belly of a specially modified B-29 bomber in his Bell X-1 rocket plane over California's Mojave Desert, Yeager lit the X-1's engine. He piloted the craft to a speed of over 600 miles per hour, making him the first person to fly faster than the speed of sound. "It was as smooth as a baby's bottom," Yeager said

later. "Grandma could be up there sipping lemonade."

Flying wasn't initially so smooth for Yeager. A native of Hamlin, West Virginia, he signed up for the Army Air Corps a month before Pearl Harbor. Taking the first flight of his life the following spring in a twin-engine bomber, he promptly got airsick and threw up. "It was," he recalled later, "a very uncomfortable situation." But once he started flying planes himself, the problem vanished, and he became a hotshot fighter pilot. He flew 64 combat missions, on one occasion shooting down five German aircraft.

The young ace had proved that he possessed all the confidence and daring the air force demanded of its test pilots. It was a hard fact that the lives of some of them would be part of the price of aeronautic progress in the brave new world of supersonic flight. Yeager survived, partly because of sheer luck and partly because he possessed, in the words of Tom Wolfe's 1979 book that made his name famous to a new generation of Americans, "the right stuff."

Yeager's stuff had staying power. On October 14, 1997, the 50th anniversary of his historic X-1 flight, the 74-year-old broke the sound barrier again, this time piloting a hot F-15 fighter.

Chuck Yeager stands beside the X-1 rocket plane, named for his wife.

Alfred Kinsey
The Statistician of Sex

The greatest biological commotion in the U.S. since Darwin." Thus did *Life* describe the reaction to Indiana University zoologist Alfred Kinsey's 1948 book, *Sexual Behavior in the Human Male*. Never before had a scientist methodically assembled and exhaustively analyzed so much data about so unmentionable a subject. Extrapolating from what 5,300 male interviewees told him, Kinsey reported that 50 percent of the nation's husbands cheated on their wives; 95 percent of all 15-year-old boys were engaged in some sort of sexual activity; 70 percent of American males had visited a prostitute; and a third of them had had homosexual experiences.

A few Americans shrugged at the news; others were titillated; many denied that Kinsey's data were accurate; and a predictable contingent of puritanical moralists savagely attacked the 54-year-old Kinsey, a friendly, rumpled workaholic who enjoyed gardening and classical music. The *Chicago Tribune*, giving voice to their attitudes, declared that he was a "real menace to society."

Kinsey took it all in stride. "Frankly," he said after the ruckus had gone on for a while, "I should think the public would be extremely tired of the subject." He himself was not, and he made a companion study of female sexuality, published in 1953. By then, Americans were getting used to, and even appreciating, the new openness about sex, for which they could thank Dr. Kinsey.

Alfred Kinsey, shown above in his book-lined Indiana study in this photograph by Arnold Newman, began amassing case histories on human sexual behavior in 1938.

"If I had any ulterior motive in making this study, it was the hope that it would make people more tolerant."

Dr. Alfred Kinsey

1948

Milton Berle
Mr. Television

A master of gender-bending gags, Milton Berle gets himself up for a skit as a jowly Cleopatra.

When Milton Berle's joke-a-second, pie-in-the-face energy first appeared like a tornado on the tiny screens of the relatively few American homes that had TV in 1948, the nation's nascent boob-tube habit took a giant leap—right into the television age. The 40-year-old Berle, a silent-film actor as a child and later a vaudeville star, was the host of NBC's *Texaco Star Theater* radio show when the network tried him out on the show's TV version in the summer of 1948, with boffo results. The show began regular telecasting on Tuesday, September 21, at 8:00 p.m., with Berle on board as host.

The chemistry was magical. Within weeks Berle's madcap hilarity had captured 94.7 percent of the nation's TV sets turned on at that hour, and, as "Uncle Miltie" himself recalled, "Crazy things started happening." An Ohio movie-theater manager put a poster in his lobby that read, "Closed Tuesday. I want to see Berle, too." In Brooklyn the owner of a laundromat installed a TV and lured customers with the slogan "Watch Berle while your clothes whirl." During the show's first year the number of sets in U.S. homes doubled; Berle was widely credited with the spurt.

"Anything for a laugh" was Berle's motto, and he kept the laughs coming on Tuesday nights for eight years. Even after his show had run its course, he remained the one and only Mr. Television.

A Cavalcade of Great Comedians

From vaudeville to movies to radio to TV, from slapstick to high wit, these comic geniuses kept the American public howling.

The Marx Brothers *Wisecracking Groucho (bottom), impish Harpo (center), and con man Chico brought their irreverent stage shtick to film in 1929's The Cocoanuts.*

Burns and Allen *George claimed that Gracie was the funny one. Teamed in 1923, they won hearts in every medium. After her death in 1964 he worked for another 30 years.*

Bob Hope *Never at a loss for a one-liner, Hope linked humor with public service. His morale-boosting tours during World War II—and ever after—made him beloved.*

Carol Burnett *Her TV show aired weekly from 1966 to 1977 and won more than 20 Emmys. Burnett combined personal warmth with parody, pratfalls, and funny faces.*

Richard Pryor *Starting with stand-up in the early 1960s, Pryor was one of the first nationally successful black comedians. His razor-sharp humor often focused on race.*

Robin Williams *A master of improvisation, Williams debuted as a lovable, manic alien in the 1978 sitcom Mork and Mindy, then starred in film drama as well as comedy.*

Rodgers and Hammerstein

Geniuses of the American Musical Theater

Long before the scheduled April 1949 opening of *South Pacific,* long before any critics could make their pronouncements, fans of musical theater were lining up to buy their tickets for this newest creation of songwriter Richard Rodgers *(below, left),* 46, and lyricist Oscar Hammerstein II *(right),* 51. The prolific pair had already scored big with smash hits *Oklahoma!* in 1943 and *Carousel* two years later, and another enchanting evening seemed certain.

Sure enough, *South Pacific* was a triumph for Rodgers and Hammerstein, who had once again transformed musical comedy into musical drama, with music, words, and dance artistically woven together. In trying to account for their extraordinary careers, Rodgers once said, "What happened between Oscar and me was almost chemical. Put the right components together, and an explosion takes place."

Mao (right) poses at his mother's funeral with, from left, his younger brother, father, and uncle. Mao said that he "learned to hate" his father.

Mao addresses a 1939 anti-Japanese rally. After Japan invaded China in 1937, he briefly allied with the Nationalists against the common enemy.

Mao rides on horseback amid his troops in 1947. A tough soldier, he survived the Communists' famous 6,000-mile Long March of 1934-1935.

1949

Mao Zedong

The Formidable Father of a New China

In the days of the Chinese empire, Beijing's Gate of Heavenly Peace was the place where momentous events of state were announced. On October 1, 1949, Mao Zedong used the same setting to proclaim the birth of a new Communist state, the People's Republic of China. Recalling the foreign economic and military interventions that had subjugated China and hastened the collapse of the Ching dynasty in 1911, Mao had a warning for the world at large: "Ours will no longer be a nation subject to insult and humiliation. The Chinese people have stood up."

It was a moment of dazzling triumph for the 55-year-old leader. After helping found the Chinese Communist Party in 1921, he had gone on to lead an army of peasants that for two decades endured incredible hardships while fighting Chiang Kai-shek's Nationalist forces for control of China, until the Communists achieved final victory.

Mao was himself a peasant by birth. Rejecting the peasant tradition of filial piety, he left home at 16 to escape his autocratic father and acquire more education. An ardent nationalist, he steeped himself in the Chinese classics, but he also absorbed the ideas of Marx and Lenin. By turns scholar and poet, visionary and pragmatist, political organizer and military leader, he was also, according to a fellow student, "arrogant, brutal, and stubborn." Mao's physician apparently concurred, writing that Mao was "devoid of human feeling, incapable of love, friendship, or warmth."

Nor did he shy away from bloodshed. When his vaunted economic experiment, the Great Leap Forward, proved a catastrophic failure, he sensed widespread disillusionment among his subordinates. Fearing loss of authority to party leaders whom he labeled revisionists, in 1966 he unleashed a ghastly bloodletting called the Cultural Revolution.

Paradoxically, the leader whose policies are now blamed for the deaths of more than 20 million of his people became the focus of a cult of personality. Always the canny politician, Mao, shown at right surrounded by apparent admirers in 1959, did nothing to discourage their adulation, since it strengthened him against potential rivals. By the time of his death in 1976, the man who once described himself as "a lone monk walking the world with a leaky umbrella" had become, to the 850 million Chinese he led, much more like a god.

Photographed in his Oxford, Mississippi, study in 1955, William Faulkner hunches over the glass-topped table at which he did most of his writing.

William Faulkner

Uncompromising Literary Voice of the South

William Faulkner often said, "I'm just a farmer who likes to tell stories." And, as it happened, he was out liming a field one fall day in 1949 when his wife, Estelle, rushed from home with the news that he had won the Nobel Prize for literature. In fact, Faulkner only played at being a farmer, but he was possibly America's greatest 20th-century storyteller. In novels and short stories he repeatedly explored the fictional Yoknapatawpha County, whose real-world counterpart was Oxford, Mississippi, where his family's roots went deep and where he spent most of his life. In his writings he elaborated over time a sprawling, tragic saga in which the burdens of the past—the tortured legacy of slavery, old family hatreds and loyalties, clashes of caste and class, violence, greed—were always present.

Success was slow in coming to Faulkner, and for a while some Oxfordians called him Count No'count, a barbed reference to his aristocratic ancestry and his spotty work history. The pessimism in his stories and the depravity of some of his characters upset many locals, as did his hard drinking. But in the end Oxford appreciated Faulkner for putting it on the literary map. When the Nobel Prize was announced, the town threw a fish fry in honor of its great native son.

Leading 20th-Century American Novelists

Whether telling tales, venting opinions, or exploring the psyche, these writers, in their novels, both reflected and influenced their culture.

Willa Cather *Writing of the American frontier, Cather peopled novels like My Antonia (1918) with strong characters who shared her attachment to the land.*

Ernest Hemingway *His revolutionary use of sparse, journalistic prose helped Hemingway win both the Pulitzer Prize and the Nobel Prize for literature.*

John Dos Passos *Combining prose with poetry, Dos Passos inserted fragments of history and pop culture into his 1936 trilogy U.S.A., a profoundly influential work.*

John Steinbeck *Voicing social protest through fiction, Steinbeck used The Grapes of Wrath, which won the 1940 Pulitzer Prize, to champion the Okies of the Depression.*

F. Scott Fitzgerald *In Fitzgerald's stories of the Jazz Age, his heroes suffered moral collapse despite social success, reflecting the dissatisfactions of the era.*

Ralph Ellison *The Invisible Man, published in 1952, made Ellison both famous and controversial. The brutally honest novel took racial identity as its central theme.*

Billy Graham, speaking at a 1957 rally, preached to over 200 million people world-wide—more than anyone else in history.

Billy Graham

Evangelist to the Whole World

In 1934 a 15-year-old North Carolina farm boy visited the tabernacle of Mordecai Fowler Ham, a revivalist preacher from Kentucky, and his life changed. "I opened up my heart then," said Billy Graham, "and knew for the first time the sweetness and joy of God, of truly being born again."

Ordained a Southern Baptist minister in 1939, Graham would devote the remainder of his life to spreading the gospel. After a spell of preaching "at every cowpath and wagon track in Florida," as he put it, he went on to conduct open-air services for returning World War II servicemen in Chicago and attracted hundreds of thousands to an eight-week crusade in Los Angeles. In 1950 he began preaching on the radio.

In 1953 Eisenhower became the first of many American presidents to seek Graham's counsel, and a year later *Time* called him "the best-known, most talked-about Christian leader in the world today, barring the Pope," and "one of the greatest religious influences of his time." But he took such accolades in stride. "If God should take His hands off my life, my lips would turn to clay," he said. "I am but a tool of God." Graham continued to tend his ministry over the next four decades, in one crusade reaching a billion people by satellite. In 1996 he and his wife, Ruth, received the Congressional Gold Medal for lifetime achievement.

Edward R. Murrow

Founding Father of Television Journalism

At Washington State College he majored in speech rather than journalism, and he had no experience as a reporter. But Edward R. Murrow's radio news broadcasts from Europe dramatically conveyed the terrors of war to Americans before Pearl Harbor. Later he almost single-handedly invented the field of television news.

Hired by CBS in 1935 to organize cultural programs, Murrow was in Poland when Germany annexed Austria in 1938. Chartering a plane to Vienna, he broadcast both the news and the sound of Nazi troops goose-stepping into the capital. For this scoop, he was made permanent correspondent in London. There Murrow developed the fearless reporting style that made him famous. While covering the Battle of Britain, he often took his microphone into the streets and let the whine of air-raid sirens and the rumble of explosions help tell the story of the German bombings. Listeners sat rapt before their radios as he intoned, "Hello America. This . . . is London."

After the war, Murrow *(inset, in 1954)* became the guiding force behind CBS radio's news bureau. He brought along his hard-hitting approach when his show *Hear It Now* was moved to TV in 1951 and renamed *See It Now*. The program followed American infantrymen on a dangerous patrol during the Korean War, looked at racism in the South, and took on the powerful redbaiting senator Joseph McCarthy *(page 115),* beginning that demagogue's downfall. Murrow also hosted the celebrity-interview program *Person to Person* and launched the documentary series *CBS Reports*.

In 1958 CBS canceled *See It Now* to make way for more profitable but vapid programming. One critic wrote, "[*See It Now*] is television's most brilliant, most decorated, most imaginative, most courageous and most important program. The fact that CBS cannot afford it but can afford 'Beat the Clock' is shocking." Murrow agreed, and a few years later he left the network in disgust. He died of lung cancer in 1965, just 57 years old.

1951

New Yorker Lucille Ball (far left) smiles for the camera with five other starlets in this Hollywood publicity shot. She gave up modeling and moved west in 1933, when she was 22. Relegated to bit parts after she arrived, she did not get a screen credit her first two years in movies.

In this scene from I Love Lucy, a pregnant Lucille Ball, playing the show's daffy heroine, faces irate Cuban bandleader husband Ricky, played by real-life Cuban bandleader Desi Arnaz, Ball's business partner and husband.

Lucille Ball
TV's All-Time Queen of Comedy

Lucille Ball's face, wrote *TV Guide,* was "seen by more people, more often, than the face of any human being who ever lived." Yet her trek to stardom required a full quarter century of struggle. It began in New York City in 1926, when she was 15. Arriving from her birthplace of Jamestown, New York, with high hopes of becoming an actress, she answered chorus call after chorus call for Broadway musicals but never made the cut. A producer's assistant, exasperated by her perseverance, once told her, "You're not meant for show business. Go home."

Ignoring the advice, Ball made some headway as a model. Then she tried Hollywood, where she had mixed success as a Goldwyn Girl and contract player for Columbia and RKO, appearing in more than 80 films. She married Desi Arnaz six months after meeting him in 1940, but the union proved rocky from the beginning; Arnaz was a playboy, and long stints on the road with his band gave him ample opportunity to indulge.

In 1947 Ball scored big with a radio sitcom, *My Favorite Husband.* When she was asked to move the show's premise to television, she saw a chance to save her marriage: She insisted that Arnaz be cast as her on-screen husband. *I Love Lucy* debuted on CBS in October 1951, and within four months became the number one show in the country. It was the first to be filmed in front of a live audience, the first to feature a Hispanic actor in a starring role, and the first to deal with pregnancy in a straightforward manner. (The 1953 episode in which Lucy gave birth to Little Ricky attracted 40 million viewers, double the number who watched President Eisenhower's inauguration the next day.) Yet the key to its success was clearly Lucy, whose hilariously expressive face *(right)* and outrageous schemes to escape from Ricky's domineering shadow entertained men and women alike.

Ball and Arnaz divorced three years after *I Love Lucy* went off the air in 1957. Lucy bought out Desi's half of Desilu, the couple's production company, becoming the first woman president of a major Hollywood studio, and went on to star in two more series, *The Lucy Show* and *Here's Lucy.*

1951

> "Marlon never really had to learn to act. He knew. Right from the start he was a universal actor."
>
> Stella Adler, Brando's drama instructor

Marlon Brando
Brilliant Bad Boy of Stage and Screen

He had been a free spirit at home, a troublemaker in school, an expellee from a Minnesota military academy. But when Marlon Brando arrived in New York City in 1943 at the age of 19, for the first time in his life he worked hard. Studying drama at the New School, he so impressed his teacher, Stella Adler, that she predicted he'd become the best young actor in America. Four years later he did just that.

As Stanley Kowalski, the brutish brother-in-law of Blanche du Bois in Tennessee Williams's *A Streetcar Named Desire,* Brando left theater patrons gasping, colleagues spellbound, and reviewers reaching for superlatives. Years later critic Richard Schickel wrote, "When the curtain came down at the Ethel Barrymore theater on Dec. 3, 1947, our standards for performance, our expectations of what an actor should offer us in the way of psychological truth and behavioral honesty, were forever changed." "It was awful and it was sublime," said a director. "Only once in a generation do you see such a thing in the theater."

Brando *(left, as Stanley Kowalski)* re-created the role in a 1951 film version, giving audiences nationwide a glimpse of the electrifying acting style that Adler labeled a "perfect marriage of intuition and intelligence" and receiving the first of four successive Oscar nominations. He won three years later for his searing performance as ex-pug-hoodlum-with-a-conscience Terry Malloy in *On the Waterfront.*

Brando sneered at the Hollywood milieu. "The only reason I'm here," he said in 1954, "is because I don't yet have the moral strength to turn down the money." But he went on to make 28 more movies, playing such diverse roles as an outlaw biker in *The Wild One,* Napoleon in *Désirée,* an Okinawan houseboy in *Teahouse of the August Moon,* and Fletcher Christian in *Mutiny on the Bounty.* He won a second Oscar in 1972 for his portrayal of Don Vito Corleone in *The Godfather.*

Premier Leading Men of Hollywood

A host of men with acting talent, memorable voices, and striking looks have knocked moviegoers' socks off since Al Jolson boasted, "You ain't heard nothing yet!" in the first full-length talkie in 1927. The eight pictured here are among the very best.

Humphrey Bogart *Star of such classics as Casablanca and Treasure of the Sierra Madre, Bogey received only one Oscar, for The African Queen (left).*

Sidney Poitier *For his work in the 1963 film Lilies of the Field (left) Poitier became the first African American ever to win the best-actor award.*

James Stewart *Whether in Mr. Smith Goes to Washington or The Man From Laramie, the versatile Stewart won hearts with his warm humor and appealing stammer.*

Paul Newman *Beginning in 1954 the blue-eyed idol starred in a score of great films. He gave riveting performances in, among others, Hud (1963) and The Verdict (1982).*

Spencer Tracy *A winner of back-to-back Oscars, Tracy made more than 60 films. Woman of the Year (left) also starred his longtime love, Katharine Hepburn.*

Jack Nicholson *A perennial favorite, Nicholson won Oscars for his performances in One Flew Over the Cuckoo's Nest (left), Terms of Endearment, and As Good as It Gets.*

Henry Fonda *The plain-spoken Nebraskan brought out the human in the hero and vice versa. He made his last film, On Golden Pond, with his daughter, Jane.*

Dustin Hoffman *No role seemed too offbeat for him— a down-and-outer in Midnight Cowboy (right), a cross-dresser in Tootsie, an autistic savant in Rain Man.*

1952

Edward L. Bernays

The Original Spin Doctor

Graduating from college with a degree in agriculture, Edward L. Bernays in 1912 seemed destined to follow in the footsteps of his father, a grain exporter. But successful stints as a publicist on Broadway and a propagandist with the government agency charged with drumming up support for America's war effort convinced him that his future lay in public relations, not agronomy.

Hired by major corporations, foreign governments, and various big shots after opening the world's first PR firm in 1919, Bernays taught generations of spin doctors how to change people's minds. He perked up President Calvin Coolidge's image by inviting Al Jolson to the White House and made Ivory soap popular by organizing a national soap-carving contest. He also increased cigarette sales by persuading women that smoking in public was daring and independent—and better for the figure than candy, which, as Bernays so cleverly suggested, spent "a moment on the lips and 10 years on the hips." His 1952 book *Public Relations* remains the bible of Madison Avenue.

1953

James Watson and Francis Crick

Solvers of Biology's Ultimate Puzzle

At midcentury biologists knew about the existence and role of DNA, deoxyribonucleic acid. But its structure—believed to hold the key to the process by which life is created from inorganic material—remained a mystery. For two years James Watson *(below, left)*, a 25-year-old Chicago-born geneticist, and Francis Crick *(below, right)*, a 37-year-old British biologist, attacked the problem.

In a Cambridge University laboratory they built model after intricate model of the DNA molecule, based on studies conducted earlier by scientist Maurice Wilkins. But they could get none of the models to square with Wilkins's data.

Finally, late in 1953, Watson and Crick hit upon a configuration that worked: a double helix, two spiral-shaped strands that wound around each other. During reproduction, the researchers theorized, one strand splits away and pairs with a single strand from another molecule, creating a copy of the original. "We have discovered the secret of life!" Crick announced jubilantly. Their breakthrough, one of the most important discoveries of 20th-century biology, earned them and Wilkins the 1962 Nobel Prize and opened the door to the promising field of genetic engineering.

Joseph McCarthy
Modern-Day Grand Inquisitor

In the years after Joseph McCarthy was elected to the Senate in 1946, Americans were jumpy about world events: The Soviets exploded an atomic bomb. Communists took power in China. An English atomic scientist was arrested for spying. Sensing opportunity, McCarthy made a speech in February 1950 that was sure to grab headlines. He held up a sheaf of papers, claiming it was a list bearing the names of 205 Communists employed by the State Department. The claim couldn't be proved, but it did its job. It soon made him one of the most powerful and unscrupulous figures of the Cold War.

McCarthy *(above, with aide Roy Cohn on the left and a staff investigator)* went on to turn government agencies upside down and ruin innocent lives in a frenzied and largely unopposed witch hunt. But when, in 1954, he accused the secretary of the army of covering up espionage, he went too far. In the ensuing televised hearings McCarthy showed that no ploy was too low for him. The Senate censured him in December, and he drank himself to death three years later.

1954

Earl Warren

Activist Leader of the Supreme Court

When he was named chief justice of the United States by President Eisenhower in 1953, Earl Warren had been California's attorney general for four years and its governor for 12, but he had never served a day as a judge. Nor had he ever expounded a philosophy of law that might offer clues as to how he would act as head of the highest court in the land. Ike selected Warren because he thought the Court needed a good administrator. What he got was an ac-

tivist chief justice who committed himself to judicial strengthening of civil rights and liberties. Over his 16-year career on the Court Warren altered relations between white and black Americans, legislators and their constituents, and police and suspects.

His Court's most famous decision, delivered on May 17, 1954, overturned a doctrine that for nearly 60 years had sanctioned racial segregation. "In the field of public education," Warren wrote in *Brown v. the Board of Education,* "the doctrine of 'separate but equal' has no place. Separate educational facilities are inherently unequal." The verdict gave new life to the civil rights movement but outraged most white Southerners—and annoyed Eisenhower, who considered race relations a local, not a federal, issue. Ike came to think of Warren's appointment as the "biggest damn fool mistake" he ever made.

Similar disgruntlement greeted Warren's revolutionary 1964 ruling that seats in state legislatures must no longer be apportioned geographically, but on the basis of population. Also hotly debated was his bold pronouncement of criminal suspects' rights in *Miranda v. State of Arizona* in 1966, three years before he retired. The case yielded guidelines—including the familiar declaration "You have a right to remain silent"—that law-enforcement officials still follow when conducting interrogations. Despite the objections, Warren left a more just nation in the wake of his service on the Court.

1955

James Dean

Hollywood Rebel No. 1— With or Without a Cause

James Dean's star flared only briefly in the cinematic firmament, but his impact, especially on teenagers, was profound. Boys copied the way he slicked back his hair, dressed, and talked. Girls gazed into his sultry, piercing eyes and longed to love him. And almost every young person in America, it seemed, understood exactly how he felt.

He got his first professional acting job—a Pepsi commercial—in 1950, the year after he graduated from high school. He started appearing in TV shows the following year. And in 1952, at age 21, he won his first role in a Broadway play. Two years later, director Elia Kazan offered him the role of Cal in the movie *East of Eden.*

Dean was already working on a second film, *Rebel Without a Cause,* when *East of Eden* opened nationwide to rave reviews on April 9, 1955, and he finished a third, *Giant,* five months after that. But he would never see it. Released from a studio contract that forbade him to take part in road races, he was driving his Porsche Spyder to a rally on September 30 when another car pulled into his path, causing a collision. Dean, estimated to have been driving at over 100 mph, was killed instantly. Just 13 days earlier he had made a public-service TV spot asking people to drive safely. "Remember," he had said with a smile, "the life you save may be mine."

Twenty-four-year-old James Dean casts his trademark smoky stare off-camera on the set of Giant, his last film, released 13 months after his death.

Martin Luther King

Conscience of a Nation

In December 1955 the Reverend Martin Luther King Jr. was a 26-year-old husband, a graduate student, the father of a newborn daughter, and the pastor of Dexter Avenue Baptist Church in Montgomery, Alabama. Few people outside his church knew much about him. But when Rosa Parks, a black seamstress, was arrested for refusing to give up her seat on a city bus to a white man, King was chosen to head a committee that organized a bus boycott to protest Parks's arrest. He not only guided the city's black community to victory but emerged as the nation's foremost black leader.

King was a student of the principles of nonviolent civil disobedience taught by Thoreau and Gandhi *(pages 50-51)*. During the course of the 381-day protest he was arrested, he received death threats, and his house was bombed, yet he urged his followers to retaliate only with the weapon of love. "We must realize," he said, "so many people are taught to hate us that they are not totally responsible for their hate."

After the successful bus boycott, King launched an all-out campaign for black civil rights, working through a new organization, the Southern Christian Leadership Conference. He pushed for desegregation and voting rights across the South, promoted lunch-counter sit-ins in 1960, advised Freedom Riders in 1961, and led marchers in Birmingham, Alabama, in early 1963. King's famous oration during the March on Washington that summer *(inset)* inspired millions around the world.

King acknowledged that his work might place him in danger. "If physical death is the price that I must pay to free my white brothers and sisters from a permanent death of the spirit," he said in 1964, the year he won the Nobel Peace Prize, "then nothing can be more redemptive." He was assassinated in Memphis on April 4, 1968.

> "This is no time to engage in the luxury of cooling off or to take the tranquilizing drug of gradualism. *Now* is the time to make real the promises of democracy."
>
> Martin Luther King Jr., August 28, 1963

Martin Luther King delivers his inspiring "I have a dream" speech from the steps of the Lincoln Memorial in Washington, D.C., on August 28, 1963. The address pricked America's conscience; Congress passed the landmark Civil Rights Act the following year.

King, shown opposite delivering a sermon, was a passionate advocate of nonviolence. "I believe that unarmed truth and unconditional love will have the final word in reality," he said in 1964. "That is why right, temporarily defeated, is stronger than evil triumphant."

Torchbearers of the Struggle for Civil Rights

Many black men and women fought for racial equality and justice in the 1950s and '60s. The eight shown below were re- *markable for their valor, sacrifice, and commitment to effecting change where it was hardest to come by and needed most.*

Rosa Parks *Her refusal to knuckle under to Jim Crow sparked a protest that touched off the civil rights movement and propelled Martin Luther King Jr. to prominence.*

Whitney Young Jr. *Head of the National Urban League from 1961 until his death in 1971, Young worked with the White House to lay the groundwork for President Johnson's War on Poverty.*

Ralph Abernathy *King's closest confidant, Abernathy assumed the presidency of the Southern Christian Leadership Conference in the painful days after his friend's assassination in 1968.*

Roy Wilkins *Through a succession of leadership positions in the National Association for the Advancement of Colored People, Wilkins devoted a half-century to promoting civil rights.*

James Farmer *A pioneer in the struggle—he cofounded the Congress of Racial Equality (CORE) back in 1942—Farmer helped organize Freedom Rides in the early 1960s.*

Fannie Lou Hamer *She fought to have black Mississippians seated at the 1964 Democratic Convention, leading to a ban on discriminatory southern delegations by both parties.*

Medgar Evers *A Mississippi NAACP official, Evers (center, below) was shot in June 1963. His murder moved President Kennedy to ask Congress for a comprehensive civil rights law.*

Stokely Carmichael *This militant Trinidadian promoted "black power" after replacing moderate John Lewis as head of the Student Non-Violent Coordinating Committee in 1965.*

Elvis Presley

The King

Teenagers turned off by the blandness of early 1950s society embraced rebels like Marlon Brando and James Dean as their idols. But the biggest idol of them all was a young singing phenomenon named Elvis Presley. A 19-year-old Memphis truckdriver, Presley got his first break in 1954 when Sun Records owner Sam Phillips invited him in for a tryout. The session was going nowhere until Presley started singing "That's All Right," an R&B number. Phillips, who had been looking for what he called a "black sound inside a white boy," realized he had a hit.

Presley's fame spread quickly. After a tour of the South, during which his pomaded locks, smoldering looks, and sexy moves knocked teen audiences for a loop and alarmed their elders, RCA Victor bought his contract. In January 1956 he recorded "Heartbreak Hotel," his first million-seller. "Blue Suede Shoes," "I Want You, I Need You, I Love You," "Hound Dog," and "Don't Be Cruel" came the same year, as did a landmark appearance on *The Ed Sullivan Show*.

Presley then made a string of mediocre movies that were huge commercial successes. Even when he went off to the army for two years in 1958, his popularity did not diminish. But during the '60s his style changed. He acquired a fleet of Cadillacs and a pretty young wife and became a Las Vegas headliner. Then the marriage collapsed, and except to perform, he seldom left the gated confines of his Memphis mansion, Graceland. His weight ballooned and he became addicted to a combination of uppers and downers. At age 42, he was found dead on the floor of his bathroom.

Eighty thousand grieving fans packed the street outside Graceland to bid him a final farewell, and in death he seemed to become more popular than ever. By the end "the King" had sold more records, scored more top-10 hits, and spent more consecutive months on the charts than any artist in history.

"I want you to know that this is a real decent, fine boy."

Variety-show host Ed Sullivan, 1957

Television viewers had never seen anything like Elvis Presley in 1956. Ed Sullivan ordered his cameramen to show the hip-swinging singer only from the waist up.

1956

Allen Ginsberg
Poetic Muse of the Beat Generation

Few American poets have provoked as much controversy in their lifetimes as Allen Ginsberg *(above)*, a core member, along with Jack Kerouac, William Burroughs, and others, of the so-called beat generation of the '50s. The 1956 publication of Ginsberg's most famous poem, "Howl"—a coarse, even vulgar meditation on the anxieties and ideals of young people cast out from mainstream America—sparked a high-profile obscenity trial that was decided in the poet's favor.

The controversy gave Ginsberg nationwide notoriety, and he never lost it. A fixture of the next decade's counterculture—he coined the phrase "flower power"—and a leader of demonstrations against the Vietnam War, he earned a spot on FBI director J. Edgar Hoover's list of dangerous subversives. Regardless of Hoover's opinion, however, Ginsberg's continued writing gained him a place in the National Institute of Arts and Letters.

1957

Theodor Geisel
The Beloved Dr. Seuss

In 1957, 53-year-old author Theodor Seuss Geisel *(below, with models of some of his characters)* could already look back on a full career. He had won Oscars for his screenplays and awards for his children's books, and Dartmouth had granted him an honorary doctorate, giving some substance to the title he had been using in his nom de plume of 20 years—Dr. Seuss. But his best was yet to come.

Asked to write a book for young readers using a vocabulary of no more than 225 words, Geisel produced *The Cat in the Hat*, a zany tale that came in two words under the limit. Told in a rollicking rhyme and illustrated with whimsical drawings, the book appealed to children everywhere—including even those who had become parents—and marked the swan song of dry, Dick-and-Jane-style books.

Leonard Bernstein

Renaissance Man of Music

The circumstances on November 14, 1943, could hardly have been more challenging: That afternoon's performance of the New York Philharmonic was to be broadcast live on radio, but the scheduled guest conductor, Bruno Walter, was too ill to appear. Leonard Bernstein, the orchestra's 25-year-old assistant conductor, would have to stand in—without a rehearsal.

One writer compared Bernstein's predicament to that of an outfielder attempting a shoestring catch in a big ball game: "Make it and you're a hero. Muff it and you're a dope." But Bernstein did not muff it; he turned in a triumphal performance that made the front page of the *New York Times* and launched his career. Ten years later he be-

came the first American to conduct at Milan's famed La Scala opera house. In 1958 he was named sole conductor and music director of the Philharmonic, the first American to hold that position with a major orchestra. And in the years to come he would take the Philharmonic traveling—to South America, Israel, Japan, and the Soviet Union.

Bernstein *(above, in rehearsal)* was a born showman, but he also made music theory and instrumentation easy to understand in his *Omnibus* programs and *Young People's Concerts* on television. He was an excellent pianist. And he won acclaim for his compositions, especially for the musical *West Side Story.* "I don't want to spend the rest of my life, as Toscanini did, studying and restudying, say, 50 pieces of music," he explained. "It would bore me to death. I want to conduct. I want to play the piano. I want to write music for Broadway and Hollywood. I want to write symphonic music. I want to keep on trying to be, in the full sense of that wonderful word, a musician."

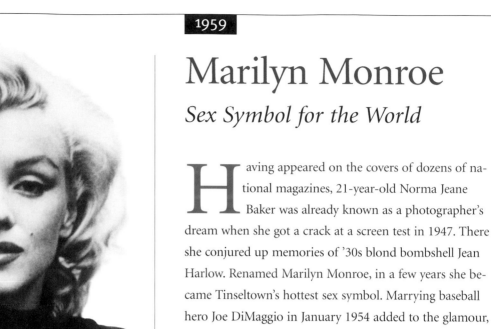

Marilyn Monroe
Sex Symbol for the World

Having appeared on the covers of dozens of national magazines, 21-year-old Norma Jeane Baker was already known as a photographer's dream when she got a crack at a screen test in 1947. There she conjured up memories of '30s blond bombshell Jean Harlow. Renamed Marilyn Monroe, in a few years she became Tinseltown's hottest sex symbol. Marrying baseball hero Joe DiMaggio in January 1954 added to the glamour, though the magical match-up didn't last out the year.

"In Hollywood's pagan pantheon," wrote *Time* magazine in 1956, "Marilyn Monroe is the Goddess of Love." A string of five movies in the mid-1950s—including the blockbusters *Gentlemen Prefer Blondes* and *How to Marry a Millionaire*—grossed over $50 million, more than any other actress of the time could claim. By 1959, when probably her best film, the comedy *Some Like It Hot*, was released, she was at the peak of her career.

Monroe's figure set a standard for her generation and, with her sparkling smile and large eyes, left male fans panting the world over. But behind that face lurked panics, fears, self-doubts—the demons of a lonely childhood spent in foster homes and an orphanage. Riotous harassment by reporters and photographers wherever she went did nothing to help. She surprised Hollywood in 1956 by marrying playwright Arthur Miller and making a bid to shake the "dumb blonde" image. Eventually, the new image took; eventually, the marriage didn't. By the time she made *The Misfits* in 1961, she was hooked on sleeping pills and prescription drugs. Increasingly troubled and alone, she was found in August 1962 in the bedroom of her Los Angeles home dead of a drug overdose. She was 36.

In this 1953 photo by Alfred Eisenstaedt, Marilyn Monroe's glamour was tempered by an underlying vulnerability.

Louis and Mary Leakey
Genealogists of Our Earliest Ancestors

Louis and Mary Leakey were an odd couple. He was a Cambridge-educated archaeologist and anthropologist, a hatcher of grand theories, a husband and father of two. She was a cigar-smoking, mostly self-taught archaeology buff with artistic talent and a penchant for fieldwork. In 1933 they talked about her illustrating one of his books, and he not only hired her but left his wife for her. They began working together, married in 1936, and for the next two decades searched for clues to the origin of *Homo sapiens* at the Olduvai Gorge in what was then Tanganyika.

According to the prevailing view, which held that humankind had originated in Asia, they were looking on the wrong continent. But Louis agreed with Charles Darwin, who had theorized that man's birthplace lay in Africa. And on a typically scorching day in 1959, Mary proved him correct. Rushing into the tent where he lay incapacitated by fever, she cried out, "I've got him! I've got him—our man!" With infinite patience and consummate care, she had uncovered a human skull that tests later revealed to be 1.75 million years old. The Leakeys named it *Zinjanthropus*—"Man From East Africa"—although it is now regarded as a form of *Australopithecus*. Hailed worldwide, the find marked the beginning of "the truly scientific study of the evolution of man," as a colleague put it, and made the Leakeys *(below)* the most famous scientist-spouses since the Curies.

Gregory Pincus
The Man Who Changed the World's Sex Life

Many researchers contributed to the creation of the family of oral contraceptives commonly referred to as the pill, but the scientist credited with directing the pill's development was endocrinologist Gregory Pincus *(inset)*. Pincus received both a master's degree and a doctorate from Harvard in 1927, at the age of 24. He then made a research specialty of reproductive physiology, and especially the relationship between ovarian hormones and sterility. In 1951 he impressed Margaret Sanger *(pages 38-39)*, the founder of Planned Parenthood, with the results of his research on animals. She arranged funding for Pincus and his team to develop an oral contraceptive for women.

Approved by the FDA for prescription use in 1960, his pill sparked a social revolution. "In a mere six years," wrote *Time* magazine—somewhat optimistically—in 1967, "it has changed and liberated the sex and family life of a large and still growing segment of the U.S. population: eventually, it promises to do the same for much of the world. . . . For if the pill can defuse the population explosion, it will go far toward eliminating hunger, want and ignorance."

A youthful John (upper left) is photographed with the rest of the Kennedy clan in 1946.

An American royal couple, Jack and Jackie pose on their wedding day, September 12, 1953.

President Kennedy eases a chronically sore back in his favorite rocking chair at the White House.

John F. and Jacqueline Kennedy

Resplendent Residents of the White House

He was the handsome, charismatic scion of a wealthy Massachusetts political family, a decorated war hero, a Pulitzer Prize-winning author, a Democratic U.S. senator, and, at age 43, the youngest man ever elected president. She was the lovely, cultured, French-speaking daughter of a well-to-do Newport, Rhode Island, family and a 1947 Queen Deb of the Year. Their 1953 wedding had been the social event of the decade. Eight years later, on Inauguration Day, John F. Kennedy and his wife, Jacqueline, became the most-watched first family in history.

Americans may have chosen Jack Kennedy over Richard Nixon by only a slim margin—118,000 of 68 million votes cast—but they fell for 31-year-old Jackie in a big way. Reporters and photographers followed her and their two children constantly, her clothes and hair styles set fashion trends, and she frequently made a bigger splash while traveling than the president did. Upon returning from a visit to France, he joked, "I am proud to have been the man who accompanied Jacqueline Kennedy to Paris."

Grave international and domestic challenges tested his presidency: A standoff between Soviet and American forces in Berlin in 1961 ended in construction of the infamous Berlin Wall. Soviet nuclear missiles were detected in Cuba in 1962, provoking one of the most harrowing crises of the entire Cold War. And America's entanglement in Vietnam grew deeper, as did the government's response to the widening civil rights movement.

Neither Vietnam nor civil rights was anywhere near being resolved when President Kennedy was assassinated in Dallas on November 22, 1963. Jackie, who was seated beside her husband in the presidential limousine as the fatal shots struck, stood next to Vice President Lyndon Johnson hours later as he took the oath of office aboard Air Force One to become the new president. Then, dressed in black, she won the respect and sympathy of the world during the president's funeral services. The brief, bright era that had been dubbed Camelot was over.

Caroline Kennedy kisses dad's cheek as mom looks on in 1960. For Caroline and John Jr., born that year, no part of the White House would be off-limits to childish antics.

1960

Fidel Castro

The West's Die-Hard Marxist

On September 26, 1960, Cuban premier Fidel Castro *(above)* entered the *Guinness Book of World Records* by outdoing himself in one of his favorite activities. He excoriated "Yankee imperialists" for an unprecedented four and a half hours in a speech before the United Nations. The dynamic 34-year-old revolutionary, who had ousted Cuban dictator Fulgencio Batista on New Year's Day 1959, had declared himself and his regime Communist shortly after coming to power and had begun a long-term alliance with the Soviet Union.

Although credited with gains in healthcare and literacy, Castro's totalitarian regime was marked by repeated failures. Cuba's centrally controlled economy, crippled by a U.S.-led trade embargo and propped up by Soviet sugar purchases, floundered. A campaign to spread Communist revolution throughout Latin America was stymied. And finally, the collapse of the Soviet Union and Eurocommunism left Castro the sole Western practitioner of a bankrupt ideology. Appearing before the Cuban people in his army fatigues on January 1, 1999, the 40th anniversary of his takeover, he asserted, somewhat hollowly, "The revolution has just begun."

1961

Ray Kroc

Impresario of Fast Food

Ray Kroc *(below)*, owner of a Chicago company that sold milkshake mixers to restaurants, noted that brothers Richard and Maurice McDonald of San Bernardino, California, had bought enough of his mixers to make 40 shakes at once. When he saw the huge profits their tiny restaurant raked in by selling only burgers, fries, and shakes, he struck a deal with them to franchise the operation. Then, in 1961, he bought it outright—name, golden arches, and all. The $2.7 million price tag seemed steep, but Kroc saw an empire in the making.

His chain stressed cleanliness, fast but friendly service, low prices, and consistency—policies taught to all franchisees during a three-week course at McDonald's Hamburger University in Illinois. By the time of Kroc's death in 1984, there were 8,300 McDonald's restaurants in America and in 33 other countries around the world.

Rachel Carson

Chronicler of Earth's Wonders and Ills

I can remember no time . . . when I didn't assume I was going to be a writer," Rachel Carson *(right)* once said. "Also, I can remember no time when I wasn't interested in the out-of-doors and the whole world of nature." In 1962, those two themes found expression in *Silent Spring*, Carson's book documenting the reckless use of pesticides—a "barrage of poison" that she believed could render the earth unlivable.

Public cries of alarm were not Carson's usual style. Born in a small Pennsylvania town in 1907, she grew up shy and studious. After a few years of teaching zoology, she took a job as a biologist with the U.S. Bureau of Fisheries. She expanded a 1937 article about oceans into a much praised book, *Under the Sea Wind,* and revisited the maritime realm in later works. One, a lyrical masterpiece called *The Sea Around Us,* spent 18 months on the bestseller lists.

The idea for *Silent Spring* came to Carson when friends reported that bird life at a Massachusetts sanctuary had been harmed by spraying to control mosquitoes. She spent more than four years gathering research to support her view that agricultural chemicals could "still the song of birds and the leaping of fish in the streams." Carson died of cancer two years after *Silent Spring* became her final bestseller; sadly, she did not live long enough to see DDT banned, in 1972, and the threat to nature eased.

1962

Bob Dylan
Bard of the Downtrodden

The future Bob Dylan at age 11.

Although his guitar playing was rudimentary and he had a nasal delivery, the 21-year-old folk singer who released his first album, *Bob Dylan*, in 1962 was unmistakably a major talent with a rare poetic gift. Dylan wasn't his real name—he was born Robert Zimmerman in Duluth, Minnesota, and grew up in the mining town of Hibbing. But in 1960 he hitchhiked to New York City to be near his idol, protest singer Woody Guthrie, and to try his luck in Greenwich Village coffeehouses. He soon snagged a recording contract under the name Bob Dylan, presumably borrowed from the Welsh poet Dylan Thomas.

In the early 1960s Dylan backed his deft poetry with guitar and harmonica *(right)* and delivered a salvo of protests against segregation, war, and poverty in classics like "Blowin' in the Wind." A music critic of the time wrote that Dylan's ability to stir audiences "is unmistakable, and stems, mainly, from the words of . . . some 200 songs he has written [about] the inequalities, danger and deceits of the 1960s." By 1964 he began moving away from protest songs, and after breaking up with a longtime girlfriend he turned to songs of love, loss, and reflection in his fifth album, *Another Side of Bob Dylan*. Simultaneously he began to leave behind acoustic music and experiment with electric instrumentation. Although there were howls of protest from folk purists that Dylan had betrayed his art, the single "Like a Rolling Stone" sold a million copies that year and helped launch a new genre of pop music called folk rock. In the 1970s and '80s he explored a broad range of material, from anguish over the breakup of his marriage to an evolving spiritual quest.

Throughout his career Dylan invariably put most of his songwriting efforts into lyrics rather than music. Set to uncomplicated melodies and sung in his plain style and mediocre but oddly compelling voice, his words reached an enormous audience. By the late 1990s he had cut more than 40 albums and sold almost 60 million copies. "Bob freed the mind the way Elvis freed the body," said rock star Bruce Springsteen at Dylan's induction into the Rock and Roll Hall of Fame in 1988. "He had the vision and the talent to make a pop song that contained the whole world."

Dylan charms civil rights workers following a 1963 Greenwood, Mississippi, benefit concert.

1963

Betty Friedan

Ideologue of the Feminist Revolution

"The problem that has no name" was how Betty Friedan *(inset)* characterized the subject of her radical 1963 bestseller, *The Feminine Mystique*. "Each suburban wife struggled with it alone. As she made the beds, shopped for groceries . . . she was afraid to ask even of herself the silent question—'Is this all?' " Why, Friedan demanded, should women be limited to the roles of wife, mother, and homemaker?

Friedan, then 42, was all those things herself—except

limited. Before marrying, having children, and moving to the New York suburbs, she had been a journalist, and she kept up her writing during her years as a housewife. *The Feminine Mystique* started out as a survey she did among her college classmates. When she turned the research into an article that revealed the frustrations felt by many women, magazine editors rejected it—so she expanded it

into a book instead. It sold three million copies. In 1966 Friedan became a founder and the first president of the National Organization for Women (NOW). Later, she helped form the National Women's Political Caucus.

As the movement scored important gains, Friedan found herself at odds with radical feminists who, in her words, promoted a "down-with-men, down-with-marriage, down-with-motherhood approach." Her writings emphasized families and advocated career flexibility for both women and men. She also focused on another target of discrimination—the elderly. Her basic message was always clear: "People are looking for meaning in their daily lives."

1964

Malcolm X

A New Voice for Black America

When Malcolm X established his own Muslim sect in Harlem in March 1964, he stated that its purpose would be to "find a common approach, a common solution, to a common problem." The problem was racism, and he had devoted his whole being to struggling with it as a minister of the Lost-Found Nation of Islam—also known as the Black Muslims. A fringe religion that advocated the creation of a separate black nation, it taught that whites were oppressors who would ultimately reap apocalyptic fruits for their evil ways. Malcolm Little, as he was born in 1925, had embraced the faith during a prison term, taking the name Malcolm X. The "X," he said, "replaces the white slave-master name imposed upon my paternal forebears by some blue-eyed devil."

For 12 years the charismatic and bitingly articulate Malcolm led recruitment efforts for the movement, encouraging black Americans to be proud of their African heritage and to lead respectable lives. He also preached that whites were to be resisted "by any means necessary"—including violence. A persuasive speaker, Malcolm attracted hundreds of new members but eventually earned the disfavor of the movement's leader, Elijah Muhammad, after accusing him of financial and sexual corruption.

During a pilgrimage to Mecca in 1964, Malcolm found himself sharing Islamic fellowship with people of all colors—including white. True Islam, he came to believe, precludes racism, "because people . . . who accept its religious principles . . . accept each other as brothers and sisters, regardless of differences in complexion." Returning home as el-Hajj Malik el-Shabazz, he founded the Organization of Afro-American Unity. But his goal of uniting blacks throughout the world would go unrealized. On February 21, 1965, at a Harlem rally, he was gunned down by three men, two of them Black Muslims.

A mesmerizing orator, Malcolm X once said, "When I speak, I speak as a <u>victim</u> of America's so-called democracy."

1965

Ralph Nader
Dauntless Defender of Consumers' Welfare

When Ralph Nader accused carmakers of sacrificing safety for profits in his 1965 book *Unsafe at Any Speed*, he incurred the hostility of America's largest company, General Motors. But instead of being intimidated, he considered it a sign of success. In the years to come he would have many such successes in his role as a David battling corporate Goliaths.

Born in Connecticut in 1934, Nader attended Harvard Law School, where he became interested in the causes of auto injuries and deaths. After briefly practicing law, he worked as a government consultant investigating car accidents. This research led to his indictment of the auto industry, a hot seller that Nader publicized on one occasion by getting behind the wheel of a bumper car *(below)*. General Motors, whose Chevrolet Corvair Nader had skewered, hired detectives to investigate his personal life—which, to their dismay, was simple to the point of asceticism. Their efforts backfired: Nader sued, and GM was forced to publicly apologize and pay him a settlement of $425,000.

Nader soon shifted into high gear as a consumer-product bloodhound, gathering a small army of students and volunteers—"Nader's Raiders"—to pursue his campaigns. His idealism, incorruptibility, and legal acumen produced important legislative reforms. He met defeats, too, but his reformist zeal never waned. As he put it, "The essence of the citizens' movement is persistence."

1966

Billie Jean King
Tennis's Woman Warrior

Winning her first singles title in 1966 at Wimbledon was only one of many triumphs in Billie Jean King's lifelong crusade for fair treatment of women in sports. "Being a woman athlete didn't mean much in the '60s," she recalled. "It was a struggle. There was no attention, no support, no structure, no money." King would be instrumental in changing all that. Born Billie Jean Moffitt in 1943, she took up tennis at the age of 11 and rose rapidly to stardom, playing mainly for the love of the game until women's tennis went professional in 1970. In 1971 she became the first woman player to earn more than $100,000 in one year, and she was number one in the world for five years, winning a staggering total of 39 Grand Slam titles, including 20 Wimbledons.

But the challenge of her life came in 1973, when she took on 55-year-old Bobby Riggs, a former champion who, though over the hill, claimed he could beat any woman, and had thus far proved it by thrashing Australia's Margaret Court, a top female player. In a match billed as "The Battle of the Sexes," King trounced her man before a television audience of nearly 50 million. "Women tennis players were the reason women athletes were accepted finally," King said in retrospect, "and I think that match was the reason for it."

Pursuing her vision of a world in which women athletes "can live their dream instead of just dream it," King helped organize the first women's professional tour, the Women's Tennis Association, the Women's Sports Foundation, and World Team Tennis.

Heroines of Sport

Barred from most sports at the start of the century because of their alleged frailty, women overcame great obstacles to gain entrée to the joys of athletic exertion and competition. The sampling of winners below would grace any hall of fame.

Babe Didrikson Zaharias
Named the greatest female athlete of the first half-century, this Texan excelled at amateur basketball and track and field, then dominated professional golf.

Olga Korbut *Bouncing into the Olympics in 1972, the nimble Soviet sprite transformed gymnastics by popularizing the sport and opening it up to younger, even more daring competitors.*

Joan Benoit Samuelson *Shy about running when young, Samuelson would halt whenever a car went by. Grown up, she broke records, and in 1984 won the first women's Olympic marathon.*

Nancy Lopez *One of the most popular golfers—male or female—of all time, the poised and powerful Lopez helped turn the women's pro tour into a big-time, big-money happening.*

Hard-charging Billie Jean King let no notions of feminine decorum curb her fierce competitiveness.

Jackie Joyner-Kersee
Called the greatest female athlete of the second half-century, Joyner-Kersee holds the world's record in the grueling seven-event heptathlon.

The Beatles

The Fab Four

After the four Liverpool lads known as the Beatles released their 1967 album *Sgt. Pepper's Lonely Hearts Club Band*, Langdon Winner, the editor of *Rolling Stone*, wrote that it was "the closest Western

Civilization has come to unity since the Congress of Vienna in 1815. . . . In every city in Europe and America the stereo systems and the radio played, 'What would you think if I sang out of tune . . .' and everyone listened." The album was a creative high point for Ringo Starr, John Lennon, Paul McCartney, and George Harrison (*below, left to right*), but they already dominated pop culture.

John had first launched the band as the Quarrymen in 1956, but not until Richard Starkey (aka Ringo) came on board in 1962 did it attain its final form. Following a series of rowdy gigs in Hamburg and Liverpool dives came the first of their many hits, "Love Me Do." Witty, irreverent, and irrepressible, the mop-haired cutups drove teenage girls to screaming rapture. The delirium spread to America in 1964 after 73 million TV viewers tuned in to their debut on *The Ed Sullivan Show*. In a few months, the country's five top-selling singles were Beatles records, and within one year 29 of their songs had made the charts. Group chemistry was their creative key. "We're all really the same person," quipped Paul.

The following years were a wild ride of world tours, consciousness-raising albums, a spiritual quest in India, and filmmaking. The group's bonds began to fray after their manager died of a sleeping-pill overdose in 1967 and John took up with avant-garde artist Yoko Ono. When they finally broke up in 1970, fans were despondent. John's murder by a deranged fan in 1980 ended any hopes for a reunion.

1967

Thurgood Marshall

Battler for Racial Justice Under Law

I believe it is the right thing to do, the right time to do it, the right man and the right place," President Lyndon Johnson declared in 1967 when he nominated Thurgood Marshall to be the first African American member of the U.S. Supreme Court. Marshall's qualifications did indeed fit the job. The great-grandson of a Maryland slave, he was born Thoroughgood Marshall in deeply segregated Baltimore in 1908. He attended the all-black Howard University Law School in Washington, D.C., because the University of Maryland excluded blacks. In 1938 he began what would turn into a 23-year career as legal counsel for the National Association for the Advancement of Colored People, arguing 32 cases before the high court on which he would eventually sit, and winning all but three. Most prominent among the successes was *Brown v. the Board of Education,* in which the Court ruled in 1954 that racial segregation in public schools violated the Constitution.

Once on the Court the tart-tongued, pragmatic Marshall kept up his fight for racial fairness and human rights. He was, however, increasingly outnumbered by more conservative colleagues during the Reagan-Bush years, and he found himself more often than not a dissenting voice. Despite failing health he hung on until 1991, telling his clerks, "If I die, prop me up and keep on voting."

Ho Chi Minh

Communist Unifier of Vietnam

One of the century's shrewdest military strategists was a diminutive man who dressed in threadbare jackets and sandals made from old tires, and whom followers affectionately called Uncle Ho. Born Nguyen That Thanh in 1890 in what would soon be the French colony of Indochina, he became a Communist in Paris in 1920. Under the name Ho Chi Minh—"Shedder of Light"—he launched a movement to drive the French out of his homeland and founded the Indochinese Communist Party. He fought against the Japanese during World War II and then against the returning French. In 1954 Ho's guerrilla forces finally routed the French, whom the United States had backed in an effort to contain Communism. But Ho's victory was incomplete. The ensuing peace agreement split the country in two—Communist North Vietnam and the American-backed South. When a promised unification was stymied by South Vietnam, Ho turned his troops loose once more, and the United States stepped up aid to the South, touching off the long and bloody Vietnam War.

In 1968 Ho launched a surprise attack during the annual Tet New Year's cease-fire. The event proved the war's turning point, for that autumn Lyndon Johnson *(pages 140-141)* halted military action in favor of peace talks. Before the talks began, however, Ho suffered a fatal heart attack. Six years later, at a final cost of hundreds of thousands of lives, Ho's vision of a unified Vietnam was fulfilled when his army marched into Saigon, the southern capital.

Showing the ravages of age and responsibility, a still-undaunted Ho Chi Minh (left) confers with Vietnamese premier Pham Van Dong in 1968.

1968

Lyndon Baines Johnson
Fatally Flawed Do-Gooder

Lyndon Johnson, shown here at age seven, was born in 1908 near the tiny Texas hill-country town of Johnson City, founded by his forebears.

A teenage Johnson displays the hubristic self-esteem that marked his adult years. He was a boisterous youth who often defied his father's wishes.

"Good evening, my fellow Americans," intoned President Lyndon Baines Johnson in a television address to the nation on March 31, 1968. After announcing a bombing halt aimed at ending the war in Vietnam and outlining a plan for peace, Johnson concluded his speech with a stunning declaration: "I shall not seek," he said, "and I will not accept, the nomination of my party for another term as your President." The unthinkable had taken place. The war that Johnson had inherited, the war over "a little piss-ant country," as he had once called Vietnam, had torn the nation apart and was now ending the presidency of its larger-than-life leader.

Johnson's announcement brought to an end a colossal political career. Elected to Congress in 1937, he used a backwoodsy charm and an insider's talent for jawboning and arm-twisting to orchestrate a meteoric rise to power. By 1951, just three years into his first senatorial term, he was named Democratic whip, and he was Senate majority leader in 1960 when savvy presidential candidate John F. Kennedy chose him as a running mate.

Lifted to the presidency by JFK's assassination in 1963, Johnson displayed a level of energy that earned him the epithet the Whirlwind President. Within months after he took command, Congress passed the Civil Rights Act of 1964, voiding many of the South's Jim Crow practices. His comprehensive domestic concept called the Great Society included a War on Poverty, the creation of Medicare, and sweeping reforms in housing and education. He won a landslide election to a full term in 1964, and by the end of his tenure Congress had passed an astounding 90 percent of the 252 bills he had submitted, many of them aimed at aiding the nation's needy.

Ultimately, however, LBJ's stubbornness and pride, the attitude that led him to declare, "I'm not going down in history as the first American President to lose a war," proved his undoing. The bewildering, tragic quagmire that was Vietnam eclipsed even the noblest of his intentions. When his time in the White House ended, he retired to his Johnson City ranch where, four years later, he died of a heart attack.

Pacing the floor of the Oval Office, a much beset and sorely troubled LBJ ponders the turbulent state of the nation and his future as president.

Unhindered in the low lunar gravity by 185 pounds of spacesuit and gear, Apollo 11 astronaut Buzz Aldrin arranges seismic-testing equipment.

Apollo 11 Astronauts

The First Men on the Moon

It was 10:56 p.m. eastern daylight time on July 20, 1969, and as what seemed like the entire population of the world watched, astronaut Neil Armstrong extended a groping, tentative foot encased in a multilayered boot from the bottom rung of a ladder on a spindly-looking craft and took, in his own immortal words, "one small step for man, one giant leap for mankind."

Minutes later, Armstrong *(below, left, in postmission quarantine),* accompanied by fellow space traveler Edwin "Buzz" Aldrin *(below, right),* had achieved something unprecedented in the history of the human race—they had walked on the Moon. While a third astronaut, *Apollo 11* pilot Michael Collins *(below, center),* was orbiting overhead in the mission's mother ship, *Columbia,* Armstrong and Aldrin had piloted a lunar exploration module named *Eagle* to the Moon's surface, where they planted a 3-by-5-foot American flag, set up a series of scientific devices, and collected samples of rock. Cavorting across the lunar landscape, even the usually taciturn Armstrong waxed poetic. "It has," he rhapsodized to his fellow earthlings back home, "a stark beauty all its own."

1969

Jim Henson

Masterly Muppeteer

One of the most unusual characters to find his way onto America's TV screens was a creature made from an old green coat and two halves of a table-tennis ball. Humble material, indeed, from which to build a TV idol, but when Kermit the Frog made his debut on *Sesame Street* in 1969 along with a hodgepodge of other endearing "Muppets," he inspired a lasting love affair among legions of viewers.

Kermit and company were the brainchildren of Maryland puppeteer Jim Henson, shown below with Kermit and another Muppet named Ernie. With their soft, mobile faces and widemouthed grins, the Muppets—a term Henson derived from combining "puppet" and "marionette"—quickly became America's favorite TV tutors, helping children learn to read, write, and count on *Sesame Street*, a program on public television. Their appeal was not restricted to the young, however. *The Muppet Show,* Henson's widely syndicated adult version of *Sesame Street*, attracted a worldwide audience of 235 million viewers.

By the time of his death in 1990 at 53, Henson had left an indelible mark on the world. As *Sesame Street*'s creator, Joan Ganz Cooney, observed, "He was our era's Charlie Chaplin, Mae West, W. C. Fields, and Marx Brothers."

1970

Pelé

Brazil's Nonpareil Master of Futebol

Even among the players on the star-spangled Brazilian 1970 World Cup championship soccer team, widely regarded as the greatest squad ever assembled, Edson Arantes do Nascimento—known the world over simply as Pelé—stood out. Graced with speed and vision, he was expert at dribbling with either foot, making it appear almost as though the ball were magically attached to his shoes as he raced down the field. Equally adept at scoring, he placed 1,220 goals in 1,253 games before he retired in 1974. So revered an international sports hero was Pelé that the president of Brazil declared him a national treasure.

A journeyman player's son, Pelé had mastered the game as a child. He joined Brazil's Santos team in 1956 at age 15 and proceeded to lead his country to three World Cup titles. But a stunning second act to an already spectacular career was yet to follow: Emerging from retirement in 1975 to join the New York Cosmos, Pelé almost single-handedly turned soccer into a popular sport in the United States. On October 1, 1977, 75,646 fans crammed Giants Stadium for his farewell game against his former Brazilian teammates. In the locker room before the game, World Heavyweight Champion Muhammad Ali conceded what the world already knew. "Now," Ali said, "there are two of the greatest."

Exhibiting the intensity that earned him the nickname Black Pearl, Pelé prepares to strike for the New York Cosmos in 1975. "He lit the fires," said the head of the U.S. Soccer Federation of the Brazilian star's contribution to American soccer.

Norman Lear
TV's Funny Rule Breaker

When an overbearing but somehow likable blue-collar bigot named Archie Bunker showed up on American TV in January 1971 complaining about "your coloreds, your Hebes, your gay homosexuals, and your broads who want to take over the world," viewers knew something amazing was happening. The new sitcom *All in the Family,* an adaptation of a British show, took on topics that American networks had long considered strictly taboo, such as homosexuality, racial stereotyping, and abortion.

The show's creator and producer, Norman Lear *(inset),* wove his own liberal political leanings into the tribulations of breadwinner Archie; his long-suffering wife, Edith; their mildly rebellious daughter, Gloria; and Gloria's annoying radical husband, Mike, better known as Meathead. And Lear did it with such panache that *All in the Family* became the top-rated program on TV for an unprecedented five straight seasons. Lear said that in watching the show, "we're swallowing just the littlest bit of truth about ourselves, and it sits there for the unconscious to toss about later." Other Lear-inspired spin-offs followed, including *Sanford and Son, Maude, Good Times,* and *The Jeffersons,* each finding its own way to stretch the bounds of what was permissible on network TV.

1972

Gloria Steinem

The Fair Face of Feminism

When Gloria Steinem and her partners launched *Ms.* magazine in 1972—after a preview issue sold out its 250,000 copies in eight days—they envisioned it as a how-to publication. "Not how to make jelly," Steinem explained, "but how to seize control of your life." Of the many feminists looking to change the world, none attracted the same kind of attention as Steinem *(below)*. The 1956 Smith College graduate had already gained prominence as a freelance journalist, although she received nearly as much attention for her looks—she was described by a reporter in 1968 as "the mini-skirted pin-up girl of the New York intelligentsia"—as she did for the articles she wrote for *Esquire* and *Vogue*.

She was also an active participant in a number of liberal causes. But when she covered a hearing on abortion reform in 1968, women's rights came into focus as her true cause. "I will never forget that night as long as I live," she later wrote. "For me, that was the moment when the light bulb began to come on." Steinem in turn illuminated feminism for many women by reassuring them that one need not be a man hater or bra burner to achieve equality with men. "We're not trading places," she once said, "we're just completing ourselves." In the decades to follow she remained involved in the women's movement—through *Ms.*, public appearances, and her own writings—and one of its most prominent figures.

1973

Norma McCorvey

Standard-Bearer of the Abortion Battle

"My name is Norma McCorvey. But you know me as 'Jane Roe,' " declared one of America's most famous plaintiffs in her 1994 autobiography. Two decades earlier her court case, known as *Roe v. Wade*, had legalized abortion across America. McCorvey had endured Texas reform schools, had been through a brief, abusive marriage at 16, and had already given up two babies for adoption. Now, still in her early 20s, she was again, in her own words, "poor and alone and pregnant."

She wanted an abortion, which was illegal in Texas and most other states. Two attorneys seeking to change the laws made her the anonymous plaintiff in a case they first took to court in 1970. The Supreme Court delivered its landmark 1973 ruling in her favor—but too late to help her. Her third baby was also given up for adoption.

McCorvey *(inset, 1989)* later came to embody the conflicts that *Roe v. Wade* provoked. In 1994 she still believed in reproductive rights; the following year she was converted by Christian antiabortionists.

Golda Meir

The Grandmother at the Helm

When Golda Meir became prime minister of Israel in 1969, some thought her too old and frail for the task. She replied, "Seventy is not a sin." Born in the Ukraine in 1898 and reared in Milwaukee, Meir emigrated to Palestine as a young woman. There she began a career in politics and served as Israel's ambassador to the U.S.S.R. before a 10-year stint as foreign minister.

Meir proved to be a popular and strong prime minister. But on October 6, 1973, the Jewish holy day of Yom Kippur, Egyptian and Syrian forces attacked Israel, catching the government and defense forces badly unprepared. For days the nation's survival seemed to hang in the balance. The political fallout prompted Meir to resign the following April. Despite the setback she remained, until her death in 1978, a key political figure at home and an important symbol worldwide as one of the first women in modern times to lead a nation.

Women at the Top

In 1900 most nations denied women any role in government. By century's end impressive personalities such as those below had held power in many countries.

Sirimavo Bandaranaike *After a 1960 election made her history's first female prime minister, she led Ceylon (later Sri Lanka) in three separate terms.*

Corazon Aquino *The murder of her husband, an opponent of the Marcos dictatorship, inspired the revolution that in 1986 won her six years as president of the Philippines.*

Indira Gandhi *This controversial daughter of Nehru had ruled India with a strong hand for nearly 20 years when she was assassinated by her own bodyguards in 1984.*

Benazir Bhutto *As military rule of Pakistan ended in 1988, she became the first woman to head a modern Islamic state, but fell from power twice under corruption charges.*

Margaret Thatcher *Taking office in 1979, the Conservative leader dismantled many Labor programs while serving longer than any prime minister in the 20th century.*

Violeta Barrios de Chamorro *Nicaraguans wearied by civil war and Marxist economic chaos turned to free elections in 1990, voting in this newspaper publisher.*

Richard Nixon, in his first House term, enjoys Washington with his wife, Pat, and baby Tricia.

Republican candidates Dwight Eisenhower and Richard Nixon celebrate their 1952 nomination.

Nixon meets with Mao Zedong in a 1972 trip to China that boldly changed U.S. foreign policy.

1974

Richard Nixon

A Legacy Scarred by Scandal

History may be more forgiving of Richard Nixon than were Americans who lived through the spectacle of Watergate. His many notable accomplishments as president included opening the door to relations with Communist China and forging arms control agreements with the Soviet Union.

Fierce determination had carried Nixon from an impoverished California childhood to law school and Congress. There his no-holds-barred style of anti-Communism drew national attention and helped him gain two terms as Dwight Eisenhower's vice president. He retreated briefly to private life after losing first the 1960 presidential race to John F. Kennedy and then a bid for the California governorship. In 1968 he came back strong, winning the Republican nomination for president and the November election.

But darker events came to overshadow Nixon's achievements. His promise of "peace with honor" in Vietnam led to a U.S. invasion of Cambodia, which sparked angry protests on American college campuses, resulting in the deaths of six students. And in his second term, scandal erupted. A botched 1972 burglary at Democratic Party offices in Washington's Watergate complex was linked to a larger "dirty tricks" campaign against Nixon's political foes. A Senate investigation turned into hearings that electrified the nation. On July 24, 1974, the Supreme Court ordered Nixon to hand over tape recordings of Oval Office conversations.

The tapes, which Nixon released after protracted legal battles, contained information that was, by his own admission, "at variance with certain of my previous statements." They also proved that he and his aides had obstructed justice, devising elaborate strategies to cover up the Watergate affair. Disgraced, Nixon appeared on TV on August 8, 1974, to declare, "I shall resign the presidency effective at noon tomorrow."

Years earlier Nixon said, referring to tactics he used against his opponent when he first ran for Congress, "Of course I knew Jerry Voorhis wasn't a communist, but I had to win. The important thing is to win." Through such ruthlessness, Nixon in the end created his own greatest defeat.

Flashing one last "victory" gesture, Richard Nixon departs from the White House on August 9, 1974. A month later, President Gerald Ford pardoned him of any wrongdoing.

1974

Muhammad Ali
The Greatest

A young Cassius Clay exults after a 1963 win with his trademark style of lyrical braggadocio.

"There will never be another like me."

Muhammad Ali

I've rassled with an alligator, I've tussled with a whale, I've done hand-cuffed lightnin' and threw thunder in jail. I'm so fast I run through a hurricane and not get wet. George Foreman is gonna pay me a debt." The debt Muhammad Ali referred to was the heavyweight boxing championship of the world. Known as the rumble in the jungle, the bout between Ali and defending champion Foreman took place on October 30, 1974, in Kinshasa, Zaire, and drew an estimated 60,000 fans. They were there to watch the self-described greatest fighter of all time regain his lost title.

Ali started out as Cassius Marcellus Clay of Louisville, Kentucky. He became a Golden Gloves winner, an 18-year-old Olympic gold medalist in 1960, then a flamboyant young world champion—who adopted a new name and a controversial new religion when he joined the Black Muslims. He successfully defended his title nine times. But in 1967 he was stripped of the championship and then sentenced to five years in prison when he refused to submit to the draft, claiming exemption as a Nation of Islam minister. Although he was eventually cleared of the charges, his vindication was not complete until he won back what mattered to him most: the heavyweight title. That he did with a new technique he called rope-a-dope, lying back against the ropes blocking punches until Foreman began to tire, then delivering an eighth-round knockout blow.

At 32, Ali was back on top. He would fend off 10 more challenges to his title, then lose and regain it again in 1978. But his lightning-fast reflexes began to slow in what proved to be the onset of Parkinson's disease, and in 1981 he retired.

Near the end of his career, Ali became a sometime statesman, undertaking several diplomatic missions to the Middle East and Africa while staying involved in social and political causes at home. By 1996, when he carried the torch at the Atlanta Olympics, the burden of his disease was clear, but his power to move a crowd remained undimmed. "I am the greatest," Ali had proclaimed from the beginning, and fans never disagreed.

Taunting his opponent by leaning on the ropes, Muhammad Ali bides his time before knocking out youthful George Foreman in a 1974 title bout.

*As time went on, hard feel-
ings over Ali's stance on
Vietnam gradually faded.
"The people . . . didn't like
the war either," he said.*

Male Sports Immortals of the Century

In endeavors where the merest of the competitors perform with a grace, skill, and courage that sets them apart from ordinary people, these men achieved levels of execution and had records of accomplishment that awed even their fellow athletes.

Jim Thorpe *Named by sportswriters the greatest male athlete of the first half-century, this Native American earned gold in the 1912 Olympics for the decathlon and pentathlon, then went on to excel in professional football and baseball.*

Bill Tilden *"Big Bill"— number one in the world from 1920 to 1925—took seven U.S. Nationals, led the U.S. to seven consecutive Davis Cups, and was the first American to win Wimbledon.*

Jesse Owens *Setting national track-and-field records in high school and world records in college, this sharecropper's son mocked Hitler's boasts of Aryan superiority by capturing four gold medals in the 1936 Berlin Olympics.*

Jim Brown *With size, speed, elusiveness, and power, the Cleveland Browns' incomparable fullback could run around or through anyone. His 1957-65 career rushing record of 12,312 yards endured into the 1980s.*

Bill Shoemaker *Shoe's gentle hands consistently coaxed the best from horses 12 times his weight. From 1949 to 1990 he booted home a world-record 8,833 winners.*

Jack Nicklaus *Cool and deliberate, he was the upstart who snatched the crown from Arnold Palmer's head in the 1962 U.S. Open and went on to become Golf magazine's Golfer of the Century.*

Wayne Gretzky *Said to score goals "nobody else even dreams about," hockey's "Great One" turned pro in 1978; by 1989 he had already glided past Gordie Howe's lifetime record of 1,850 points.*

Steven Spielberg
Master of Box-Office Magic

In 1961, Boy Scout Spielberg (right) could already be found behind the camera: "From age 12 or 13," he said, "I knew I wanted to be a movie director."

Summer 1975 was the "summer of the shark." The blockbuster *Jaws* lured moviegoers in droves while unnerving beachgoers, marking a triumph for 27-year-old director Steven Spielberg. But by then he was already a veteran behind the camera. As a 12-year-old, he used his family's 8-mm camera to make a film, complete with script and cast. "Our living room was strewn with cables and floodlights," recalled his mother. "We never had a chance to say no. Steven didn't understand that word."

At 17 Spielberg spent a summer watching and learning at Universal Pictures, but on a less-than-official basis: "I found an office that wasn't being used," he said, "and became a squatter." He came back to Universal a few years later to show executives one of his short films and was soon directing television programs and TV movies. In 1974, his first studio film, *The Sugarland Express*, proved a box-office disappointment. But it was a skillfully made, well-reviewed film that paved the way for *Jaws*, the breakthrough event in his career.

After that, Spielberg turned almost everything he touched into cinematic gold. A steady march of blockbusters, including *Close Encounters of the Third Kind, Raiders of the Lost Ark, ET: The Extra-Terrestrial,* and *Jurassic Park* made him the most successful moviemaker of all time. In 1994 *Schindler's List,* the haunting black-and-white tale of the Holocaust, won Spielberg his first Oscar as best director. It was a film he had to make, Spielberg said, but one that marked a departure from his previous work. "My movies are usually so much about fantasy," he explained. "Here . . . history is much more extreme than anything I could possibly dream up." Another historical film, *Saving Private Ryan,* brought Spielberg his second best-director Oscar in 1999.

Directing is "what I do best," said Spielberg (above, on location in 1980). "I love the work the way Patton loved the stink of battle."

Throughout his work, Spielberg saw a constant theme. "What binds my films together," he said, "is the concept of loneliness and isolation and being pursued by all the forces of character and nature."

Jimmy Carter
Outsider in the White House

I 'll never tell a lie," Jimmy Carter assured voters in 1976. "I'll never betray your trust." Character and integrity were as much a part of Carter's platform as any political issue, and he proudly termed himself an "outsider." In many ways, that was exactly the word for the born-again Baptist and farmer. And for better or worse, he remained an outsider throughout his presidency.

James Earl Carter Jr. had been a navy officer serving on nuclear submarines until his father died in 1953. He then returned to Plains, Georgia, to run the family peanut farm and warehouse business. In 1962 he won election to the state legislature and then, in 1970, served a term as governor before launching his presidential bid.

Carter supported the Equal Rights Amendment and praised the civil rights acts of the 1960s. He also vowed to streamline the federal government and encourage free enterprise. This combination of liberal and conservative appeal won him just over half the popular vote against incumbent Gerald Ford. After the election, Carter set the tone of a presidency for the people. He banned the playing of *Hail to the Chief* as too regal, sent daughter Amy to public school, and turned White House thermostats down to 65 degrees.

Carter scored some notable achievements in foreign policy, including treaties on the Panama Canal and the near-miraculous Egypt-Israel peace accord. But his domestic performance was far less successful. He had poor rapport with Congress. High unemployment, rampant inflation, and soaring oil prices, inherited from previous administrations, set off a deep recession on his watch. But it was his inability to cope with the Iranian hostage crisis, when 52 American embassy staff were kidnapped in November 1979 by a government-backed Tehran mob and held for 444 days, that doomed his chances of reelection.

After leaving the White House, Carter helped build low-income housing, promoted peace in troubled regions of the world, and furthered humanitarian causes through his Carter Center in Atlanta. In many ways his accomplishments in retirement outshone his presidency.

In keeping with Carter's plain-folks style, the first family eschewed a limousine and walked down Pennsylvania Avenue on Inauguration Day.

Anwar el-Sadat of Egypt (above, left) and Israel's Menachem Begin (right) clasp hands with Carter in March 1979 after signing the peace agreement he had brokered the year before at Camp David.

On the campaign trail in 1976, Carter returns home for services at Plains Baptist Church and flashes his familiar grin while posing with a less-than-enthusiastic baby.

1977

Wozniak and Jobs

The Men at the Core of Apple

One was passionate about computer design, the other had a gift for marketing. Together they launched the personal-computing revolution in 1977. Steve Wozniak *(above left, with the first Apple computer)* and Steve Jobs *(right)* met at electronics giant Hewlett-Packard. Both wanted to develop an affordable home computer. At first they planned to make only a printed circuit board that customers could buy for about $50 and expand at home. But a retailer offered to take 50 fully assembled computers at $500 apiece. "That was the biggest single episode in the company's history," recalled Wozniak.

Jobs sold his Volkswagen bus, Wozniak his programmable calculator, and with the resulting $1,300 they began operating from a spare bedroom. Calling themselves Apple Computer—partly in homage to the Beatles' record label—the pair produced their first computer in 1976. By then, Wozniak was already designing a more advanced machine. The Apple II, launched in 1977, became the first mass market personal computer and a huge bestseller. Within four years, Jobs and Wozniak had a $1.3 billion corporation.

1978

John Paul II

The Pope From Poland

Un Papa straniero!"—"A foreign Pope!"—shouted a surprised crowd in Rome when Karol Wojtyla, born in Wadowice, Poland, was elected to the papacy in 1978. But the warmth and exuberance of the first non-Italian pontiff in four and a half centuries soon prevailed. John Paul II became the most traveled pope in history, attracting enthusiastic throngs the world over. A 1981 assassination attempt slowed his pace only briefly.

Wojtyla came of age during the Nazi occupation of Poland. A laborer by day, he was active in the resistance, helping Jews to safety. Neighbors recalled that after the death of his widower father, the grief-stricken young man spent 12 hours in prayer. Soon he began secret studies for the priesthood, and in 1946 he was ordained.

Father Wojtyla rose quickly. As archbishop of Cracow, he was a formidable adversary for Poland's Communist government, but in his papal writings on social and economic justice he often took capitalism to task as well. Unyielding on church doctrine—"You cannot take a vote on the truth," he once said—John Paul gained both critics and adherents, but no one could deny his popular appeal.

Mother Teresa
Missionary of Compassion

As a child, Mother Teresa—born Agnes Gonxha Bojaxhiu of Albanian descent in Skopje, Macedonia—would accompany her mother on errands of mercy. "When you do good," her mother instructed, "do it quietly, as if you were throwing a stone into the sea." Agnes took the lesson to heart for the rest of her life, and in 1979 her good works were honored at the highest worldly level—she was awarded the Nobel Peace Prize for her "compassion without condescension."

The girl her brother recalled as "fun-loving and mischievous" became a nun in 1928, at age 18. After nearly 20 years as a teacher in Calcutta, India, she formed the Order of the Missionaries of Charity to help India's flood tide of poor. The order grew to encompass more than 500 clinics, hospices, orphanages, and homes for lepers, the mentally ill, and the aged.

Mother Teresa's response to the Nobel Prize? "Personally, I am unworthy," she said. "I accept in the name of the poor." Then she requested that the customary banquet be canceled and the money donated to the needy.

1980

Ronald Reagan
An Actor on the World Stage

"Dutch" Reagan (third from left, with parents and brother Neil) grew up in small-town Illinois.

"As government expands, liberty contracts."

Ronald Reagan, 1989

ogether we are going to do what has to be done," Ronald Reagan declared after being elected president in 1980. "We're going to put America back to work." For voters who had struggled through a decade of bad news—Vietnam, Watergate, economic woes, the Iran hostage crisis—Reagan exerted strong appeal. Part of it was the optimism he radiated and his nostalgic, almost mythical vision of America; part was his heartfelt, sincere, and passionate delivery. It wooed voters much as it had won fans for him during his days in radio and on the screen.

Although Reagan had been a liberal, he became concerned about Communism after World War II and testified before the House Un-American Activities Committee about Communists in Hollywood. Then, as host of television's General Electric Theater, he visited GE plants to tout the virtues of private enterprise. Eventually, he became a full-time Republican activist, and in 1965 he ran for governor. After two terms in the California statehouse, he decided to aim for the presidency. "The longer I had been governor," he explained, "the more I realized the biggest problems regarding Big Government had to be solved in Washington."

As president, Reagan carried out his major campaign promises: increasing military spending, cutting taxes and government programs, and taking a tough stance toward the Soviet Union—the "evil empire," in his words. The high points of his eight years in office included an ebullient economic recovery and a landmark 1987 arms reduction treaty with the Soviets. Many historians also gave him major credit for the collapse of the U.S.S.R. and European Communism.

But he had failures as well. The federal debt spiraled ever upward during his administrations. Income disparity shot up too, while the homeless became a familiar sight on American streets. Secret arms sales to Iran and illegal covert aid to the Nicaraguan Contras shocked the public. Those revelations failed, however, to make a dent in Reagan's reputation. His enduring popularity—often mystifying to commentators—was in many ways his single greatest achievement.

In a typically upbeat mood, Reagan laughs at a quip made by Queen Elizabeth II during her 1983 visit to the United States.

Ronald and Nancy Reagan relax in the White House movie theater. Their California ranch, however, was "where I restore myself," Reagan said.

Lech Walesa

Instigator of Polish Democracy

I had something in me that made me the leader of the gang," recalled Lech Walesa (pronounced va-WEN-sa) about his youth in the village of Popow. "I was always on top." Not so his homeland: Poland emerged from the German occupation of World War II only to find itself under Soviet control. Its people suffered under the hated Communist regime but could do little about it. Finally, in July 1980, workers at the vast Lenin Shipyard in Gdansk went on strike after the government raised meat prices. Walesa, a 36-year-old electrician and political activist, took charge. As strikes spread nationwide in August, Walesa ne-

gotiated with the government on behalf of the workers, winning the right to form independent trade unions and to strike. A new union, Solidarity, emerged and quickly gained 10 million members. But in December 1981 the government imposed martial law, jailing Walesa and other Solidarity leaders. A year later the union was outlawed.

Solidarity went underground, but the union and its dynamic leader remained potent national symbols. By the late 1980s, Soviet premier Mikhail Gorbachev's reforms signaled change for the other nations of the Communist bloc. Popular dissent and a deepening economic crisis in Poland forced the government to loosen its hold. In 1989 it permitted free legislative elections that gave Solidarity a sweeping victory and doomed Communist control. A new era of political freedom had begun in Poland. The next year Walesa was elected president, a post he held until 1995.

Ted Turner

News Entrepreneur

Skeptics called it the Chicken Noodle Network when it debuted in 1980. But CNN—the 24-hour Cable News Network—flourished with its new approach to presenting the news. The brainchild of Ted Turner *(right, at his Georgia home)*, CNN offered constant live coverage of events around the world, allowing history to unfold instantaneously before a worldwide audience. CNN was often first on the scene, and during the 1991 Gulf War even commanders and fighter pilots turned to it to track the progress of the conflict.

Turner, the son of an ambitious owner of a billboard business, took over the company after his father's suicide. He went on to create a broadcast empire that included the Turner Broadcasting System, CNN, and the TNT movie channel while earning the nickname Captain Outrageous for his unexpected business moves. His gambles on purchasing the Atlanta Braves baseball team and the MGM movie archives paid surprising dividends. Then in 1995 he startled the business world again, with plans to merge his holdings with those of media giant Time Warner. Outside the world of business Turner made headlines as well, skippering his yacht *Courageous* to an America's Cup victory in 1977, marrying actress Jane Fonda in 1991, and donating $1 billion to the U.N. in 1997. Of his success Turner said, "A visionary is supposed to have a vision of the future. I think I was right most of the time."

Bill Gates

The Richest Person in the World

I can do anything if I put my mind to it," Bill Gates *(inset, right, with business partner Paul Allen)* once told a reporter. And few who watched his rise from computer hacker to CEO of Microsoft Corporation, the world's largest computer-software company, could deny his boast. In 1981 Gates, then a 26-year-old Harvard dropout, and his friend Allen made the most of the nascent revolution in personal computing when they licensed the use of MS-DOS, their computer-operating system, to IBM, while retaining ownership of the system. Not surprisingly, almost all the manufacturers of "IBM clones"—less expensive versions of Big Blue's PC—adopted MS-DOS as well, and Microsoft was soon a household word. By the late 1990s more than 90 percent of the world's computers ran on Microsoft Windows, a graphical version of MS-DOS using screen icons and a mouse.

The ubiquity of Windows and of Microsoft applications such as word-processing software, spreadsheets, and Internet Web browsers made Gates the world's richest person, with a fortune estimated at $70 billion. But the business tactics of the fiercely competitive CEO brought on accusations of unfair and monopolistic practices from the U.S. government and many smaller companies that had to deal with Microsoft to ensure that its products would be compatible with theirs. Said one of Gates's former employees, "He's relentless. Success is defined as flattening the competition." Still, while Gates was often vilified by industry insiders as a conniver and a bully, his larger public image became that of a modern Horatio Alger, a self-made success.

Paul Allen, incredibly wealthy in his own right, eventually left Microsoft, but he continued to sit on its board of directors and to serve as a touchstone for his old friend. The two would reminisce, Gates said, "about how the fantasies we had as kids actually came true."

Michael Jackson

Pop Music Mega-Thriller

Ever since I was a little boy," wrote Michael Jackson in 1988, "I had dreamed of creating the biggest-selling record of all time." Jackson's dream began taking shape when he was only five, fronting his brothers in an act their father managed called the Jackson 5. Motown Records signed the group in 1968, and by age 12 *(inset)* Jackson had a slew of hits.

Parting ways musically with his family at 21, he went solo, and with the release of his second album in 1982 his childhood wish came true: *Thriller* sold more than 40 million copies and won eight Grammys. Jackson's videos of the title track and the singles "Billy Jean" and "Beat It" set new standards of artistry and excitement, and his riveting "moonwalk" and offbeat costumes inspired major fashion trends.

As Jackson continued to dazzle the public, the media turned ugly at times, exposing his unconventional personal life—including his friendships with young boys and his brief marriage to Lisa Marie Presley, the daughter of the late Elvis. The shy star was driven into near seclusion at his Neverland Ranch in California, scarcely emerging except for performances.

In the 1987 video Bad, Jackson displays a mesmerizing array of self-taught choreography skills.

Sally Ride

A Woman With the Right Stuff

I didn't come into the space program to be the first woman in space," said 32-year-old Sally Ride, who did become America's first female astronaut. "I came to get a chance to fly as soon as I could." Nevertheless, her June 18, 1983, flight aboard the space shuttle *Challenger* spoke volumes about the progress of American women.

A star college tennis player, Ride was urged to go pro. Choosing graduate school instead, she studied physics and astrophysics, and when NASA began recruiting astronaut-scientists in 1978 after a hiatus of nearly a decade, she was selected. Along with four male crew members, Ride *(below, during a sleep period in space)* shared the shuttle's cramped quarters for six days. After touchdown she exclaimed, "I'm sure that's the most fun I'll ever have in my life."

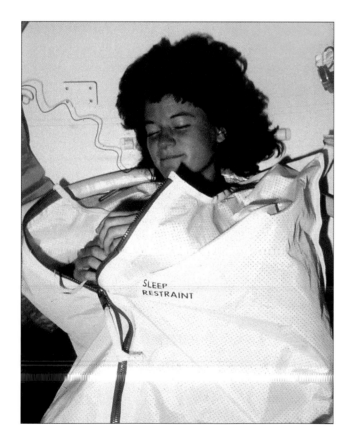

SLEEP RESTRAINT

Desmond Tutu

South Africa's Bishop of Peace

One of my greatest sadnesses is that there are many in this country who are not joining in celebrating something that is an honor for this country," said South Africa's Anglican bishop Desmond Mpilo Tutu when he accepted the 1984 Nobel Peace Prize. Many white South Africans had in fact reacted with anger at his selection, and a white-owned daily paper remarked that the bishop's frequent "outbursts" made him "an unlikely peace-prize recipient." But Tutu knew the true merit of the tribute: "The award is a tremendous political statement," he declared. "It says that despite all distortion of truth, the world recognizes that we are striving for peace."

Tutu had spent his life working for a nonviolent end to apartheid, South Africa's brutally racist social system. Under apartheid, blacks, denied virtually all democratic rights, forced into the worst jobs for low pay, and confined to crowded, disease-ridden slums, lived lives little better than slavery. They rebelled in the 1960s, beginning a long siege of civil strife that would leave thousands dead.

Tutu *(right)*, ordained an Anglican minister in 1961, used the power of the pulpit to speak out against apartheid —and against violence. In 1985 he was appointed bishop of Johannesburg, and at great personal risk pleaded with other nations for support in the antiapartheid campaign, calling for economic sanctions to force the government to abolish its barbaric practices. A year later the U.S. Congress responded, imposing sanctions.

The campaign finally bore fruit with the 1989 election of F. W. de Klerk, when the government began to adopt radical reforms. Blacks gained the vote in 1993 and wielded it enthusiastically in South Africa's first free elections in 1994, choosing as the nation's leader Nelson Mandela *(pages 178-179)*. Tutu remained a strong influence, playing an invaluable role as a watchdog over the new government.

1984

> "I don't think you can bring the races together by joking about the differences between them. I'd rather talk about the similarities. . . ."
>
> Bill Cosby

Bill Cosby

America's TV Father

"I am your father. I brought you into this world and I can take you out." Spoken with a deadpan delivery by funnyman Bill Cosby to one of the errant children on his TV sitcom, such startling lines convulsed the show's huge audience. But when *The Cosby Show* debuted in September 1984, its parent network, NBC, had low expectations for it. Cosby had insisted on total creative control, and NBC thought the resulting program lacked the urban edginess that audiences would expect from a sitcom about a black family.

What the network didn't realize was that the show, based largely on Cosby's own family life, appealed to the common humanity of the audience. Almost unnoticed was its unprecedented portrayal of a nonstereotypical African American family who were affluent, intelligent, and happy together. The show earned eight Emmy nominations and held the number one spot in the ratings for four consecutive years.

Born in 1937, Cosby learned early that he could make life easier by telling tall tales. A teacher's note on a report card said, "William should become either a lawyer or an actor because he lies so well." While attending college on an athletic scholarship, he discovered that his talent could pay when he filled in for the regular comedy act at a local club. He quit college in 1962 to make a career of comedy, basing much of his act on childhood memories. In 1964 he became the first African American to star in a prime-time television drama, *I Spy*, and by 1969 he had earned five Grammys for comedy albums.

After *The Cosby Show* shut down in 1992 at the end of its eighth successful season, Cosby continued his career with live appearances and TV shows and as pitchman for a variety of products. Tragedy struck in 1997 when his only son, Ennis, was murdered. For many of Cosby's fans, it felt almost like a personal loss.

Ryan White
Youthful Model of Courage

In the early 1980s the baffling new affliction called AIDS brought with it a plague of terror and misunderstanding. It took the courage of a frail young boy to slay the ugly specter of irrational fear surrounding the deadly disease. "I came face to face with death at age thirteen," said Ryan White *(below, right),* a hemophiliac who had contracted the human immunodeficiency virus (HIV) when he was treated with an infected supply of factor VIII, a product made from donated blood. He was diagnosed with AIDS in 1984.

Ryan's mother, Jeanne, sued the company that made factor VIII, and the local news media picked up her story. Soon the Whites began to sense that they were no longer welcome around Ryan's hometown of Kokomo, Indiana. They had become the targets of a kind of bigotry based on fear. At church they were forced to sit alone. Restaurants isolated them, then threw away their dishes when they left. Finally, school officials said that Ryan could no longer attend his school. "We have to fight, Mom," said Ryan. "What they want to do isn't right. We can't let it happen to anyone else."

Jeanne took the school to court, citing medical evidence that the chances of Ryan's infecting another student were infinitesimal. The family's home was vandalized. Their car's tires were slashed. A citizens' group even petitioned to have Jeanne declared an unfit mother and to make Ryan a ward of the court. Once again the media took an interest. "Sometimes we felt like reporters were the only company we had," remembered Ryan. This time the publicity helped the Whites. The quiet dignity of their struggle was shown worldwide on television. In the meantime, on April 10, 1985, a judge ruled that Ryan could return to his school.

"Being back at school was almost as lonely as being home," said Ryan of the cruel ostracism he experienced. Returning home one day the family found a bullet hole in their front window. Ryan had had enough. "I don't want to die in Kokomo," he told his mother. "And I don't want to be buried here either." Financial support that flowed in from around the world allowed the Whites to move about 25 miles south to Cicero, where well-informed, caring citizens welcomed them with open arms. There Ryan happily turned to more normal teenage interests, such as collecting action figures, comic books, and most importantly, new friends. But on April 8, 1990, after five years of struggle, he finally lost the battle. The Ryan White Foundation, with Jeanne at its head, was established in Ryan's memory; its mission—to educate the public about AIDS.

1986

Oprah Winfrey

Queen of Talk TV

In 1986 *The Oprah Winfrey Show* went national, and within a year its 32-year-old host, shown below in 1993, was the undisputed queen of daytime TV. Oprah's rise to fame grew out of a professional fiasco. Hired as a TV news co-anchor in 1976, she had trouble coming across as a hard-nosed, objective reporter. She was reassigned to a spot on a morning chat show and discovered that it was the perfect venue for her intimate style of interviewing. "They put me on the talk show just to get rid of me," she recalled of her first day. "I came off the air, and I knew that was what I was supposed to do."

Oprah had endured a stormy childhood marked by sexual abuse, rape, and the death of a baby she bore at age 14. On her talk show she revealed her tragic history and invited her TV guests to do the same. "The show has been great for me," she admitted "I've never had a day of therapy."

1987

Mikhail Gorbachev

Would-Be Rejuvenator of the Soviet State

The most perilous moment for a bad government is when it seeks to mend its ways," wrote historian Alexis de Tocqueville. He was referring to the French Revolution, but he could just as easily have been describing the brief but spectacular career of reformist Soviet leader Mikhail Gorbachev.

Born to a family of peasant farmers, Gorbachev was bright and talented and rose rapidly through Communist Party ranks. In 1985 he became general secretary of the Party, at 54 the youngest man except for Stalin ever to lead the Soviet Union. When he came to power, his country, despite its military might, could not feed its own people, and Gorbachev set out to effect a "revolutionary renovation of socialism."

He signed a treaty with the U.S. in 1987 to scrap intermediate-range nuclear missiles, reducing defense spending to allow increased production of consumer goods. He instituted *glasnost* (openness), a radical policy that abolished the practice of official lying, permitted citizens and the press to discuss what didn't work and why, and opened state elections to non-Party candidates. "This is an evening of dancing," remarked one Russian journalist, "in a society that has never danced." Then he introduced *perestroika* (restructuring), injecting into the stagnant and corrupt Communist economic system some free-market notions of work and reward. Almost inevitably the new-style regime loosened the reins on its Eastern European satellites, and Communist dictatorships fell in quick succession in Hungary, East Germany, Czechoslovakia, and Bulgaria.

As change followed change, it became increasingly evident that the Soviet Union's problems were too deeply rooted for improvements to happen overnight. While designer clothing and perfume shops had sprung up in Moscow, everyday necessities were still scarce, and the promised benefits of reform remained only promises. Public criticism of Gorbachev escalated, reaching a peak in August 1991, when Communist hard-liners attempted a coup. Gorbachev was overshadowed by Russian Republic president Boris Yeltsin—a radical reformer elected under *glasnost*—who stood up to and foiled the plotters. Having opened the door to the future, Gorbachev yielded to the democratic sentiments that were sweeping the country and resigned from office, sounding the death knell of the Soviet Union.

At the Washington summit of the superpowers in 1987, Mikhail Gorbachev faces his American counterpart, Ronald Reagan, who praised Gorbachev's policies of glasnost and perestroika.

A close associate of Martin Luther King Jr., Jesse Jackson (left) stands with King and the Reverend Ralph Abernathy on a balcony at the Lorraine Motel in Memphis on April 3, 1968. The next day King was killed as he stood on the same balcony.

"We sit here together, a rainbow, a coalition— the sons and daughters of slave masters and the sons and daughters of slaves sitting together around a common table, to decide the direction of our party and our country."

Jesse Jackson, 1988 Democratic Convention

1988

Jesse Jackson
Tireless Spokesman for the Disadvantaged

It came as no surprise when, three years after making the first serious run by an African American candidate for the Democratic presidential nomination, Jesse Jackson stated once more, "I want to be the President of the United States of America." What was a surprise was how close he came to actually winning the 1988 nomination. In a field of seven contenders he finished second only to Massachusetts governor Michael Dukakis.

Jackson's success in the Democratic primaries that year owed much to the tireless voter-registration efforts of his National Rainbow Coalition, an organization devoted to empowering the poor, the marginalized, and the disenfranchised through political action. But the real appeal of the effort flowed directly from the candidate *(on campaign in Delaware, right)*, whose fiery oratory style had brought an army of new voters into his tent.

Jackson was born in 1941 to unwed parents in South Carolina, and the taunts of children who called him "a nobody who had no daddy" bred in him a strong awareness of injustice. While a senior in college he began organizing civil rights marches, sit-ins, and boycotts of businesses that refused to serve blacks, and in 1966 he joined the Southern Christian Leadership Conference, crusading alongside Dr. Martin Luther King Jr. Ordained a Baptist minister in 1968, he worked to empower the black community and to inspire cooperation between the races, founding an organization called PUSH—People United to Save Humanity—in 1971.

Jackson won international renown as well, speaking out against apartheid in South Africa, convincing Cuban leader Fidel Castro to release a group of political prisoners, and—perhaps most spectacularly— talking Iraqi dictator Saddam Hussein into freeing nearly 300 American and other hostages during the Persian Gulf crisis in 1990. In 1992 he urged African Americans to support presidential candidate Bill Clinton, and their votes helped put a Democrat into the White House for the first time in 12 years.

Jackson's life was itself a reflection of his own message: "People who are victimized may not be responsible for being down," he said, "but they must be responsible for getting up. . . . Change has always been led by those who spirits were bigger than their circumstances."

A low achiever as a youth, Colin Powell, shown here in 1990, was appointed to the highest office in the United States armed forces.

Colin Powell

First Black Joint Chiefs Chairman

When President George Bush tapped 52-year-old General Colin Powell to lead the Joint Chiefs of Staff in 1989, he passed over more than a dozen more-senior officers. But Powell, the first African American—and the youngest man—ever to attain the nation's highest military office, proved the wisdom of Bush's decision. Only months into his tenure he organized a lightning-fast military intervention that ousted Panama dictator Manuel Noriega. "In a performance that left politicians and viewers marveling," wrote a reporter, Powell calmly offered the country a televised explanation of the invasion.

A year later Powell won even greater praise for his impeccable judgment and superb leadership during Operations Desert Shield and Desert Storm—a joint effort by a U.S.-led coalition of countries to expel invading Iraqi forces from Kuwait. When Iraqi dictator Saddam Hussein proved intractable, Powell and American field commander General Norman Schwarzkopf directed the troops in a speedy and successful ground offensive in February 1991.

The son of Jamaican immigrants who settled in New York City, Powell had grown up more fascinated by street life than by school. Finally finding his calling in the Reserve Officers Training Corps in college, he rose quickly through the army's ranks, serving with distinction in numerous posts worldwide, including two tours in Vietnam. As chairman of the Joint Chiefs of Staff, Powell believed his position sent a positive message to African American youth. "I've made myself very accessible to the Black press," he said, "and I do that as a way of just showing people, 'Hey, look at that dude. He came out of the South Bronx. If he got out, why can't I?' "

When Powell retired from command in 1993, the Republican Party tried to persuade him to run for vice president on Bob Dole's ticket in the 1996 election, but an even louder cry went up for him to go for the top spot himself. He chose instead to work as an advocate for education among the disadvantaged and the poor, believing that, despite his indifferent efforts as a student, his years in public school had prepared him for success in a way that hard work alone never could have. "If the Statue of Liberty opened the gateway to this country," he said, "public education opened the door to attainment here."

Jack Kevorkian

Suicide Doctor

In 1990, facing inevitable death, a woman named Janet Adkins engaged Dr. Jack Kevorkian and his lethal-drug-dispensing apparatus *(below)* to hasten her end. Her death set off a nationwide firestorm of intense debate over the rights of the terminally ill and the practice of euthanasia through doctor-assisted suicide.

Kevorkian received hundreds of letters begging for his help. He challenged state laws by assisting in additional suicides, and was often put on trial—though always acquitted. Refusing to give up, he said, "It may not happen in my lifetime, but my opponents are going to lose. There's a lot of human misery out there." But his coarse manner and use of macabre humor made it easy for opponents to vilify him as "Dr. Death," and in 1999, in Michigan, he was finally convicted of second-degree murder and sentenced to 10 to 25 years in prison.

1991

George Bush
Gulf War Commander in Chief

The son of a Connecticut senator, George Herbert Walker Bush was flying navy torpedo bombers in World War II before his 20th birthday. Back from the war, he earned a Yale degree and became a Texas oilman, then began a steady rise in Republican politics leading finally to the White House. After his election in 1988, Bush ran into tough going on domestic issues. The Democrats controlled Congress, and the right wing of his own party was demanding concessions while withholding its trust. Most galling of all, he was forced to back off from his famous campaign promise: "Read my lips. No new taxes."

By background Bush preferred dealing with foreign policy. He had been ambassador to the United Nations, chief minister to China, and CIA director before becoming Reagan's vice president in 1981. And, indeed, international matters provided triumph after triumph for him in the White House. His term coincided with the breakup of the Soviet bloc in Eastern Europe and the 1991 collapse of the U.S.S.R., ending the reign of Russian Communism and leaving the U.S. the victor in the 45-year-long Cold War.

In the midst of these events, on August 1, 1990, Iraq's Saddam Hussein invaded oil-rich Kuwait. Bush *(above, greeting U.S. troops in Saudi Arabia)* built a coalition of 28 nations determined to liberate Kuwait by force if Hussein failed to withdraw by January 15, 1991. Hussein refused to move, and the Persian Gulf War began the day after the deadline. Following 40 days of American-led air attacks, a scant 100 hours of ground war was enough to drive Hussein's forces out of Kuwait and devastate his army.

The president now stood victorious, invoking American leadership in a "new world order." But Hussein managed to remain in power, and back home domestic issues again began chipping away at Bush's newfound popularity. His reelection had seemed a foregone conclusion in the heady days after the war, but in 1992 it eluded him.

Boris Yeltsin

First Leader of the New Russia

Boris Nikolayevich Yeltsin had shown a taste for challenging authority as early as his Siberian school days. Years later, in 1988, he lost his Communist Party leadership post for urging a faster pace of reform. But the next year, in a historic open election, he gained a seat in the new Soviet parliament with 89 percent of the vote. By now the brash populist was a folk hero, and in June 1991 voters confirmed Yeltsin *(below, with supporters)* as the Russian Republic's president—the first freely elected head of state in Russian history.

That August, when hard-liners tried to oust Soviet leader Mikhail Gorbachev, Yeltsin climbed atop an armored truck outside Russian Republic headquarters in Moscow and called for mass resistance. Tens of thousands joined him over the following days. "We will hold out as long as we have to, to remove this junta from power," Yeltsin declared. The coup dissolved, and then so did the Soviet Union itself, as most of its 15 republics began to break away. Gorbachev, presiding over a Communist empire that no longer existed, stepped down in December, and Yeltsin

was now head of an independent, democratic Russia.

His popularity began to erode as Russia grappled with rampant corruption and economic collapse. He survived another insurgency in October 1993 and a bloody war with the secessionist region of Chechnya. He was reelected in 1996, but his health was failing and he wavered on reform, weakening his political hold. Yet Yeltsin's position in history was secure: He was the man who had delivered the *coup de grâce* to the Soviet Communist tyranny.

Anita Hill

Dramatizer of the Sexual Harassment Issue

In October 1991, during confirmation hearings for Supreme Court nominee Clarence Thomas, University of Oklahoma law professor Anita Hill testified before the Senate Judiciary Committee. She described lewd remarks that, she alleged, Thomas had often directed at her when he was her boss at the Equal Employment Opportunity Commission 10 years earlier. Thomas vehemently denied all charges, calling the proceedings a "high-tech lynching."

Many of Hill's senatorial interrogators discounted her story, suggesting that she was emotionally disturbed or a pawn for groups opposed to Thomas. The Senate went on to confirm Thomas by a 52-48 vote. But Hill's testimony brought new attention to workplace sexual harassment, emboldening many women to speak out about their own experiences. It also helped inspire women to run for office in record numbers the next year. And the Equal Employment Opportunity Commission handled 50 percent more sexual harassment claims in 1992 than it had the year before.

1992

Slobodan Milosevic

Engine of Ethnic Hatred

Serbian president Slobodan Milosevic, leader of the dominant republic of the six that made up Yugoslavia, came to power in 1989 as an aggressive nationalist, promoting a vision of a "greater Serbia." He drew on ancient ethnic and religious hatreds to inflame Orthodox Christian Serbs against any separatist notions among the country's other republics, with their large populations of Catholics and Muslims. Then, in 1991, with the fall of European Communism, the Yugoslav federation began unraveling, and by 1992 Croatia, Bosnia-Hercegovina, Slovenia, and Macedonia had declared their independence.

With antagonisms in the region boiling over, the bloodiest conflict in Europe since World War II erupted in April 1992. Milosevic *(above, in 1995)* pleaded blamelessness, but outside observers saw his hand behind local Serb militias that massacred and uprooted Bosnian Muslims and Croatian Catholics in vicious episodes of "ethnic cleansing."

In 1995 U.N. sanctions forced Milosevic into a tenuous peace agreement. But in 1999 he launched another round of ethnic cleansing, this time against the largely Albanian Muslim population of Serbia's breakaway Kosovo province, provoking armed intervention by a U.S.-led NATO force.

1992

Rodney King

Center of a Racial Storm

A bystander with a video camera recorded a scene on March 3, 1991, that would be televised over and over in the months to come: a black man on the ground, and four white Los Angeles policemen kicking him and pounding him with their night sticks—56 blows in 81 seconds. For many it was evidence of chronic police mistreatment of African Americans. When pulled over for speeding, an intoxicated Rodney King *(below, with injuries)* had at first resisted arrest, but the tape indicated that the kicking and clubbing went on long after he lay helpless.

Most Americans expected convictions in the ensuing police brutality trial, but on April 29, 1992, a jury in overwhelmingly white Simi Valley declared all four officers not guilty. "They gave us nothing, nothing," lamented the Reverend Cecil Murray of L.A.'s First A.M.E Church. "Not even a bone, dear God, not even a bone." As thousands of black L.A. residents erupted in violent outrage, the police responded slowly and inefficiently. The result was the worst riot in 20th-century American history. More than 50 people died; fires blazed for five days. King appeared on television to plead, "Stop making it horrible. . . . Can we all get along?" A year later, two of the officers were convicted of violating King's civil rights.

Yitzhak Rabin

A Lifelong Soldier Who Chose Peace

On September 13, 1993, Israeli prime minister Yitzhak Rabin and Yasser Arafat, chairman of the Palestine Liberation Organization (PLO), stood before the White House with Bill Clinton *(above)* and shook hands. The longtime foes had just signed accords, secretly brokered in Oslo, Norway, that brought new hope for peace in the Middle East. Rabin then issued a plea to all sides in the conflict: "Enough of blood and tears!"

The Oslo Accords called for growing Palestinian autonomy in the West Bank and the Gaza Strip, land won by Israel in the 1967 Six-Day War. Rabin had masterminded that war, the highlight of his long military career. Perhaps only such a proven defender of the nation could persuade his fellow Israelis to trade territory for promises of peace. The effort earned him the 1994 Nobel Peace Prize, shared with Arafat and Israeli foreign minister Shimon Peres. But the following year Rabin was assassinated by a Jewish extremist.

Yasser Arafat

Guerrilla Turned Politician

As agreed in the Oslo Accords, on September 13, 1993, PLO chairman Yasser Arafat officially recognized Israel. The 1948 war that had won Israel's independence had left Palestinian Arabs stateless. Arafat, a student at the time, joined a campaign of guerrilla warfare against Israel. By 1969 he was head of the PLO—and despised by Israelis as a terrorist. Israeli prime minister Yitzhak Rabin defended his negotiations with Arafat by arguing that allies do not need to make peace, only enemies do.

Arafat faced bitter opposition from extremists on his own side, but like Rabin he had come to see compromise as a practical necessity. In the accords Israel recognized the PLO, while Arafat agreed to end guerrilla attacks against Israel and accepted a plan for gradual Palestinian autonomy. Of coexistence he said, "There is no other alternative." His challenge now was to govern the territory and to suppress die-hard terrorist factions among his people.

1993

Toni Morrison
A Rich American Voice

Born Chloe Anthony Wofford in Lorain, Ohio, Toni Morrison *(below)* was an English professor and editor before publishing her first novel, *The Bluest Eye,* in 1970. In this and later works—among them *Beloved,* the 1988 Pulitzer Prize winner—she wrote of black women and men in America. Her poetic style, vivid even when intricately complex, used shifts in time and perspective to represent history that had gone unacknowledged and harrowing experiences that her characters struggled to master.

In 1993, Morrison became the first African American to receive the Nobel Prize for literature. In her acceptance speech she cited Lincoln's Gettysburg Address for its refusal to be a "final word" or a "summing up," for its "deference to the uncapturability of the life it mourns. . . . Language can never 'pin down' slavery, genocide, war. . . . Its force, its felicity, is in its reach toward the ineffable."

1994

Nelson Mandela
The Prisoner Who Freed His Nation

Nelson Mandela of South Africa was destined at his birth in 1918 for leadership: He was the son of a royal family of the Xhosa people. But as a young man he chose instead life as a Johannesburg attorney and then became involved in the leading anti-apartheid organization, the African National Congress (ANC). At first he espoused nonviolent resistance to the oppression blacks faced. But by 1960, as the apartheid system grew more violent, Mandela *(inset, 1961)*

launched an ANC sabotage campaign. In 1964 he was sentenced to life in prison.

Mandela managed to resist the humiliations and dangers of imprisonment, holding on to the belief that one day he would be free. "Any man or institution that tries to rob me of my dignity will lose," he wrote in a note smuggled out by friends. Over time he grew into a figure of immense moral authority.

Meanwhile, South Africa had become a pariah state. Meeting black protests with growing brutality, it provoked costly international economic sanctions. Under this pressure, hard-line president P. W. Botha agreed to a suggestion Mandela made in 1986 that they begin a dialogue. Their secret talks, though producing no concrete action, were the first small step toward a negotiated settlement of the country's racial crisis.

Botha's successor, F. W. de Klerk, saw even more clearly the need for change. On February 11, 1990, he freed Mandela, by then the world's most famous political prisoner. Upon his release, Mandela, 71, repeated the words he spoke at his 1964 trial: "I have fought against white domination, and I have fought against black domination. I have cherished the idea of a democratic and free society."

De Klerk and Mandela then began the difficult process of negotiating the new shape their nation would take, and in 1993 they shared the Nobel Peace Prize for their efforts. The first election open to all races was held on April 27, 1994, and Mandela became president of a truly democratic South Africa. The task of reconciliation and reconstruction he faced was immense, but no greater than the stunning changes that in a few short years had freed millions of his suffering people.

Nelson Mandela appears with supporters during his 1994 campaign. On election day, black South Africans waited in mile-long lines to cast their ballots.

1995

Timothy McVeigh

A Terrorist in the Heartland

At the height of morning rush hour on April 19, 1995, the nine-story Alfred P. Murrah Federal Building in Oklahoma City was blown up by a powerful bomb *(below)*. Shock waves spread outward for 30 miles, and glass shards and masonry debris rained down. Immediately, people began digging through the rubble to rescue survivors and recover bodies. The final death toll was 168, including 19 children from the building's day-care center. It was the worst act of terrorism ever committed in the U.S.

Less than two hours later a man named Timothy McVeigh was stopped in Perry, 60 miles north of Oklahoma City, for driving a vehicle with no license plates. The police took him in when they found he was carrying a concealed pistol. Five minutes before he was to appear in court—and possibly be released on bail—the sheriff got an urgent call from the FBI: McVeigh was a suspect in the bombing.

The 29-year-old McVeigh, a recipient of the Bronze Star for service in the Gulf War, proved to have links to the far-right militia movement. He and a friend, Terry Nichols, believed that the U.S. government had become a totalitarian regime, seeing proof in the federal siege of the Branch Davidian compound near Waco, Texas. According to prosecutors it was to mark the second anniversary of the government's deadly raid on the cult that McVeigh and Nichols inflicted their homemade bomb—a rented truck filled with a fertilizer-fuel oil mix—on the Murrah building.

McVeigh *(inset)* was convicted in 1997 of murder and conspiracy and sentenced to death. Nichols, found guilty on lesser charges, was sentenced to life in prison without parole.

O. J. Simpson

Fallen Hero

He had long been a star, first as a running back for the University of Southern California Trojans and then for the Buffalo Bills, and later as a movie actor and advertising pitchman. But for most of 1995 O. J. Simpson appeared in a very different role on TV sets across America, standing trial for the vicious stabbing murders of his

glamorous ex-wife, Nicole Brown Simpson, and her friend Ron Goldman.

The two bodies were discovered just past midnight on June 13, 1994, outside Nicole's Los Angeles townhouse. After four days of police investigation accompanied by wild media speculation, an arrest warrant was issued for Simpson, triggering a bizarre, low-speed L.A. freeway chase that was telecast live around the world. Police cars and news helicopters followed Simpson's white Ford Bronco as he lay in the backseat threatening to shoot himself. Eventually Simpson surrendered to police.

The trial, broadcast live on television, lasted for eight months. Prosecutors believed they had a strong circumstantial case buttressed with DNA evidence and proof that Simpson had physically attacked Nicole and harassed and threatened her. But the "dream team" of defense lawyers created reasonable doubt in the minds of the jurors. In particular they alleged that detectives, motivated by racism, had tampered with the evidence.

On October 3, to the glee of many African Americans and the disgust of many whites, Simpson *(shown here in happier times with Nicole and their children, Sydney and Justin)* was acquitted. He later lost a wrongful-death lawsuit brought by the victims' families. The case and the verdict were notable for what they revealed about race relations in America, spousal abuse, and the rules of evidence in criminal cases.

Ian Wilmut

The Father of Cloning

It took almost 300 attempts, but in 1996 Ian Wilmut at Scotland's Roslin Institute achieved a historic scientific breakthrough: the birth of a cloned lamb. Created with a cell from an adult ewe, Dolly, as she was named, was an exact genetic replica of her mother. Scientists had produced animal clones using fetal cells before, but never one from an adult cell. Publication of Wilmut's findings in the magazine *Nature* set off a frenzy of reactions, mostly concerning the ethics of cloning. Could humans be cloned, the world wondered?

Nature's editors thought human cloning possible within a decade. Wilmut *(below, with Dolly)* argued that it should not be attempted. "We have some hard thinking ahead of us," said Harold Shapiro, head of a presidential committee studying the issue. Meanwhile, Dolly proved no fluke; a Japanese researcher soon produced litters of cloned mice.

1997

Princess Diana
The People's Princess

Diana gazes lovingly at Prince Charles on their wedding day in 1981. The princess wore 40 yards of English silk and a 25-foot train.

In 1988 the princess poses with the great loves of her life, sons William, top, and Harry. She tried hard to give them a normal childhood.

Lady Diana Spencer became an object of popular fascination as soon as word of her relationship with Charles, Prince of Wales, leaked during the summer of 1980. By the time the couple's engagement was announced in February 1981, the shy but photogenic 19-year-old was known around the globe. Five months later, 750 million viewers watched the royal wedding on TV.

The marriage appeared to be the stuff of fairy tales, and especially so when the princess promptly satisfied her dynastic obligations by producing the next generation's heir to the throne: Prince William, born in June 1982. William's brother, Prince Harry, arrived in 1984. But in fact it was an unhappy union. Charles had married out of a sense of obligation, not love. And lacking Diana's warmth and *joie de vivre,* so obvious in the 1989 photo at right, he came to resent the attention the media showered on his wife and the admiration so lavishly bestowed on her by the public.

Amid nonstop worldwide headline treatment, the couple separated in 1992 and divorced four years later. Diana lost the title "Her Royal Highness" but remained Princess of Wales, received a multimillion-dollar settlement, and, more important to her, retained the right to share in her sons' upbringing. Reports of new romantic involvements for Diana appeared in the press, mixed with accounts of her reaching out compassionately to suffering and downtrodden people around the world. When she and her Egyptian boyfriend Dodi al-Fayed were killed in a car crash in Paris on August 31, 1997, the question of whether she had finally found true love went unanswered.

Grieving millions watched on TV as her coffin was solemnly borne to Westminster Abbey on September 6. "She was the people's princess," British prime minister John Major said, "and that is how she will stay in our hearts and memories forever."

Michael Jordan takes to the air with a soaring slam dunk in the decisive sixth game of the 1998 NBA Finals.

Michael Jordan

The Best There Ever Was

When Michael Jordan retired in 1998 after 13 NBA seasons, he was widely considered the finest player the game of basketball had ever seen. "If there is a heaven on earth, it certainly includes a vision of Jordan at the height of his powers," wrote Frank Deford in *Sports Illustrated* that year. "He made sport into art in a way that we really haven't seen . . . since the Greeks chose athletes, foremost, to decorate their amphoras." Jordan's accomplishments were astonishing. He made a last-second jump shot to win a national championship for the University of North Carolina in 1982. He led the United States to Olympic gold medals in 1984 and 1992. And he turned the once-hapless Chicago Bulls into the

dominant team of the '90s, twice leading them to three consecutive championships, securing the final title with his final shot of his final game. Fans took it for granted that had he not left the NBA for almost two seasons—following the brutal murder of his father—to try his hand at baseball, his Bulls would have posted eight straight titles.

Even Jordan's rivals marveled at his abilities. Boston Celtics great Larry Bird went so far as to call him "God disguised as Michael Jordan." But it was Nike, the giant athletic shoe company, that gave scope to his godlike effects off the court. When the company introduced Air Jordan shoes in 1984, his first pro season, it hoped sales would reach $3 million in three years. But thanks to His Airness, who was named Rookie of the Year, Nike sold more than $130 million worth in that year alone.

Endorsement deals with other corporations soon followed, proving that Jordan's appeal extended beyond sports and transcended race. Stylish and handsome *(inset)*, and more lovable, according to surveys, than even avuncular retired newsman Walter Cronkite, Jordan became what one observer called "the greatest corporate pitchman of all time."

His fame also made him the highest-paid athlete ever and led to appearances on TV shows and a starring role in the 1996 movie *Space Jam*. Yet he never disappointed those who wanted to be like Mike. "In a world where celebrity wannabes feel they have a right to be whiny and boorish," wrote Deford, "Jordan has been remarkably dignified."

John Glenn

Enduring Possessor of the Right Stuff

Few people have what it takes to become astronauts, and of those who do, even fewer actually get to go into space. John Glenn remained among the elect longer than anyone. He became the first American in orbit when the Cold War was at its fiercest and Soviet achievements were making Americans fear that they would soon sleep under a Russian Moon. Flying alone in *Friendship 7*, Glenn, age 40, circled the earth three times on February 20, 1962, restaking his country's claim to the final frontier. American footprints had been on the Moon for 29 years and Glenn had been a U.S. senator for 24 by the time he made his second trip, as a payload specialist aboard the shuttle *Discovery* in 1998 *(below)*. Selected to participate in studies on the effects of weightlessness on older people, the 77-year-old raised the spirits of a graying nation.

1999

Bill Clinton

First President From the Baby Boom Generation

Bill Clinton's greatest gift, according to observers, was his ability to communicate with average Americans. "No one who has ever seen him work a rope line or entertain questions at a town meeting can fail to be impressed by the way he engages with ordinary people," wrote the *New York Times.* His magnetism was said to rival that of his idol, John F. Kennedy, whom a 16-year-old Clinton met on a visit

to the White House in 1963 *(inset).* Thirteen years later, Arkansans elected Clinton attorney general, and two years after that, when he was 32, they made him the nation's youngest governor. Turned out in 1980, he reclaimed the office in 1982 and held it until 1992, when voters nationwide chose him over 68-year-old George Bush as president.

"They rejected the last President shaped by the moral universe of World War II in favor of a man formed by the sibling jostles and herdings of the baby boom and the vastly different historical pageant of the '60s," wrote *Time.* Clinton had tried marijuana. He had avoided the draft during the Vietnam War. And he had acknowledged having committed adultery. Yet he won.

In 1994 questions arose about the role he and First Lady Hillary Rodham Clinton

(left, in Botswana in 1998) had played in a failed Arkansas real estate venture called Whitewater. Congress appointed an independent counsel, Kenneth Starr, to investigate. By 1996, when Clinton became the first Democratic president since Franklin Roosevelt to be reelected, Starr's probe had turned up little. During that period, however, a former Arkansas state employee named Paula Jones, with financial backing from a right-wing think tank, filed suit against the president, alleging he had sexually harassed her when he was governor.

Then, in January 1998, a Pentagon employee came forward with audiotapes on which a former White House intern named Monica Lewinsky described having a sexual relationship with the president. At first Clinton denied the charges—both to the media and in depositions given in the Paula Jones lawsuit. But later, as Starr prepared a report detailing numerous Oval Office trysts, Clinton admitted that he and Lewinsky had had what he termed an inappropriate relationship.

House Republicans, crying perjury and obstruction of justice, pushed through a vote of impeachment, but most Americans just shrugged. "To a public that had already accepted Clinton with his faults," wrote the *New York Times*, "the Starr report arrived not as a shocking indictment, but as a juicy soap opera with footnotes." Almost two-thirds of voters, polls revealed, opposed impeachment, and an equal number gave his performance as president high marks, not least because of the robust national economy. Following the public's lead, the Senate, on February 12, 1999, voted to acquit.

ACKNOWLEDGMENTS

The editors wish to thank the following individuals and institutions for their valuable assistance in the preparation of this volume:
Margaret Adamic, Disney Publishing Group, Burbank, Calif.; Dr. Russell Adams, Howard University, Washington, D.C.; Richard Conn, Labor Hall of Fame, Washington, D.C.; Tom Conroy, Movie Still Archives, Harrison, Nebr; Lenore DeKoven, Columbia University, New York; Joyce Devlin, Mount Holyoke College, South Hadley, Mass.; Danielle Frizzi, Gillette Co., Boston; Mike Gentry, NASA/Media Services, Houston, Tex.; Cyndy Gilley, Do You Graphics, Woodbine, Md.; Margaret Humphreys, PhD, Duke University, Durham, N.C.; Mary Ison and staff, Library of Congress, Washington, D.C.; Frank Lentricchia, Duke University, Durham, N.C.; Jane Lowenthal, Barnard College, New York; Janice Madhu, George Eastman House, Rochester, N.Y.; John Parascandola, PhD, U.S. Public Health Service, Rockville, Md.; John Shostrom, *Sports Illustrated,* New York; Anthony Slide, Studio City, Calif.; Milo Stewart Jr., National Baseball Hall of Fame and Museum, Cooperstown, N.Y.; Carol Travers, Polaroid Corp., Cambridge, Mass.; Frank Turaj, PhD, American University, Washington, D.C.; Tim Wiles, National Baseball Hall of Fame and Museum, Cooperstown, N.Y.

PICTURE CREDITS

The sources for the illustrations in this book appear below. Credits from left to right are separated by semicolons, from top to bottom by dashes.
Cover and dust jacket: Donald C. Uhrbrock/*Life* Magazine © Time Inc.; CORBIS/Bettmann; Yousuf Karsh/Woodfin Camp & Associates, New York; CORBIS/Bettmann; Photofest, New York; Yousuf Karsh/Woodfin Camp & Associates, New York; David E. Kluths, Indianapolis, Ind.—Philippe Halsman © Halsman Estate. **3:** CORBIS. **6:** Sigmund Freud Copyrights/Mary Evans Picture Library, London—© Edmund Engelman. **7:** CORBIS/Bettmann. **8:** John Mulholland collection. **9:** Museum of the City of New York/Archive Photos, New York. **10, 11:** The Granger Collection, New York. **12:** CORBIS/Bettmann. **13:** CORBIS/Underwood & Underwood. **14, 15:** Brown Brothers, Sterling, Pa.—Culver Pictures, New York. **16:** Brown Brothers, Sterling, Pa.—Culver Pictures, New York—The Granger Collection, New York. **17:** Brown Brothers, Sterling, Pa. **18:** Hebrew University, Jerusalem. **19:** Santa Barbara Historical Society—CORBIS/Bettmann. **20:** Brown Brothers, Sterling, Pa. **21:** RMN-Picasso ©1999 Estate of Pablo Picasso/Artists Rights Society (ARS), New York; © 1998 The Museum of Modern Art, New York, acquired through the Lillie P. Bliss Bequest. Photograph © 1998 The Museum of Modern Art, New York. © 1999 Estate of Pablo Picasso/ARS, New York. **22:** Gjon Mili/*Life* Magazine © Time Inc. **23:** Hulton Getty/Liaison Agency, New York; Matisse, Henri, *Dance* (first version). Paris (March 1909) Oil on canvas, 8'6½" x 12'9½" (259.7 x 390.1 cm) The Museum of Modern Art, New York. Gift of Nelson A. Rockefeller in honor of Alfred H. Barr, Jr. Photograph © 1999 The Museum of Modern Art, New York. © 1999 Succession H. Matisse, Paris/ARS, New York; Martha Holmes/*Life* Magazine © Time Inc.; Jackson Pollock, Number 1, 1950 *Lavender Mist,* Ailsa Mellon Bruce Fund. © 1998 Board of Trustees, National Gallery of Art, Washington, D.C. © 1999 Pollock-Krasner Foundation/ARS, New York—CORBIS/Bettmann; CORBIS/Philadelphia Museum of Art © 1999 ARS, New York/ADAGP, Paris/Estate of Marcel Duchamp; CORBIS/Malcolm Lubliner; Robert Rauschenberg, *Bed* (1955), combine painting: oil and pencil on pillow, quilt, and sheet on wood supports, 6'3¾" x 31½" x 8" (191.1 x 80 x 20.3 cm). The Museum of Modern Art, New York. Gift of Leo Castelli in honor of Alfred H. Barr, Jr. Photograph © 1999 The Museum of Modern Art, New York—CORBIS/Bettmann; CORBIS/Philadelphia Museum of Art © 1999 ARS, New York/ADAGP, Paris; CORBIS/Bettmann; © 1999 Andy Warhol Foundation for the Visual Arts/Art Resource/ARS, New York. **24, 25:** Brown Brothers, Sterling, Pa. **26:** CORBIS/Underwood & Underwood—collection Michel Roudillon/photograph by Philippe Tarabella. **27:** Courtesy The Gillette Company, Boston, Mass. (2); courtesy Polaroid Corporate Archives, Cambridge, Mass. (2)—CORBIS/Bettmann; Yves Debraine, Lausanne, Switzerland; Dr. Jeremy Burgess/Science Photo Library/Photo Researchers, New York—CORBIS/Bettmann; Nike, Inc., Beaverton, Oreg. (2) **28:** Photographs & Prints Division, Schomburg Center for Research in Black Culture, The New York Public Library, Astor, Lenox and Tilden Foundations. **29:** No credit. **30:** The Frank Lloyd Wright Home and Studio Foundation, Oak Park, Ill. (H&SH167)—© Scott Frances, Esto. **31:** Alfred Eisenstaedt/*Life* Magazine © Time Inc. **32:** Limot/Archive Photos, New York; Ezra Stoller © Esto; CORBIS/Oscar White; Ezra Stoller © Esto—Ezra Stoller © Esto; CORBIS/Bettmann; photo by Matt Wargo, courtesy Venturi, Scott Brown and Associates, Inc., Philadelphia, Pa.; photo by John T. Miller, courtesy Venturi, Scott Brown and Associates, Inc., Philadelphia, Pa.—AP/Wide World Photos; Grant Mudford, Los Angeles, Calif.; George Lange/CORBIS/Outline Press; © Jeff Goldberg/Esto. **33:** Keystone View. **34:** CORBIS/Bettmann. **35:** Archive Photos, New York. **36, 37:** Culver Pictures, New York. **38:** CORBIS/Bettmann. **39:** Archive Photos, New York. **40:** Culver Pictures, New York; Witzel/MPTV, Van Nuys, Calif.; Photofest, New York. **41:** Bentley Historical Library, University of Michigan, Ann Arbor, Mich. **42:** CORBIS/Frank Driggs. **43:** CORBIS/Bettmann (3) [illegible] Orleans, La.; Hulton Getty/Liaison Agency, New York—CORBIS/Bettmann. **44:** Ria-Novosti/Sovfoto, New York. **45:** Itar-Tass/Sovfoto, New York. **46:** Culver Pictures, New York. **47:** Hulton Getty/Liaison Agency, New York. **48:** Marie Hansen/*Life* Magazine © Time Inc. **49:** Culver Pictures, New York; no credit—Brown Brothers, Sterling, Pa.; Hank Walker/*Life* Magazine © Time Inc.—CORBIS/Bettmann. **50, 51:** CORBIS/Bettmann; Margaret Bourke-White/*Life* Magazine © Time Inc. **52:** Berenice Abbott/Commerce Graphics, Ltd., Inc. **53:** Camera Press, London; *The Times*, London/Archive Photos, New York—Hulton Getty/Liaison Agency, New York (2). **54:** Yale University Library, from *Henry R. Luce* by Robert E. Herzstein © 1994 Robert E. Herzstein; Yousuf Karsh/Woodfin Camp & Associates, New York—© 1923 Time Inc.; *Fortune* Magazine © 1930 Time Inc.—Margaret Bourke-White/*Life* Magazine © Time Inc.; Mark Kauffman/*Sports Illustrated* © Time Inc. **55:** Courtesy George Eastman House. Reprinted with permission of Joanna T. Steichen. **56, 57:** Brown Brothers, Sterling, Pa. **58:** Barnard College Archives, New York. **59:** Institute for Intercultural Studies, Inc., New York. **60:** CORBIS/Bettmann. **61:** Culver Pictures, New York. **62:** Brown Brothers, Sterling, Pa. **63:** CORBIS/Bettmann (5); Reuters/Mike Blake/Archive Photos, New York—Lovero/*Sports Illustrated;* Herb Scharfman/*Sports Illustrated*. **64:** Imperial College School of Medicine at St. Mary's, London. **65:** CORBIS/Bettmann; Bill Eppridge/*Life* Magazine © Time Inc.—Wellcome Institute Library, London; David Strick/CORBIS/Outline Press—CORBIS/Bettmann; Ted Thai/*Time* Magazine—© Redding/Sipa Press, New York; J. P. Owen/Black Star, New York. **66:** © The Observatories of the Carnegie Institution of Washington; Archive Photos, New York. **67:** Library of Congress Neg. No. USZ62-37768/901911. **68:** Clarence S. Bull/Kobal Collection, New York. **69:** Movie Still Archives, Harrison, Nebr. (2)—Kobal Collection, New York; Everett Collection, New York—Mary Ellen Mark, New York. **70:** Brown Brothers, Sterling, Pa. (2)—Culver Pictures, New York. **71:** George Skadding/*Life* Magazine © Time Inc. **72:** National Archives Neg. No. 208 FS 3874-2. **73:** Brown Brothers, Sterling, Pa.; Bundesarchiv, Koblenz (4). **74, 75:** Heinrich Hoffmann; CORBIS/Bettmann; ABBAS/Sipa Press, New York—Gamma Presse Images/Liaison Agency, New York; Eddie Adams, New York. **76:** MOMA Film Archives, New York. **77:** Barbara Morgan-Morgan Press. **78:** Clinedinst Studio, Washington, D.C. **79:** Yousuf Karsh/Woodfin Camp & Associates, New York. **80:** Yale Joel/*Life* Magazine © Time Inc. Used by permission from Disney Enterprises, Inc.—© Disney Enterprises, Inc. **81:** © Disney Enterprises, Inc. **82, 83:** Archive Photos, New York; CITIZEN KANE © 1941 Turner Entertainment Co. All rights reserved. **84:** Courtesy Sinatra Family Collection—© Peter Martin, courtesy Stephanie Corley, Oakview, Calif. **85:** Herb Gehr/*Life* Magazine © Time Inc. **86:** Brown Brothers, Sterling, Pa.—Hulton Getty/Liaison Agency, New York. **87:** Yousuf Karsh/Woodfin Camp & Associates, New York. **88:** Alfred Eisenstaedt/*Life* Magazine © Time Inc. **89:** Philippe Halsman © Halsman Estate—Los Alamos National Laboratory; The Cousteau Society, Paris. **90:** Courtesy, Dwight D. Eisenhower Library, Abilene, Kans. **91:** Yousuf Karsh/Woodfin Camp & Associates, New York. **92:** Bob Landry/*Life* Magazine © Time Inc.—U.S. Army photo courtesy the Patton Museum, Fort Knox, Kent.—Margaret Bourke White/*Life* Magazine © Time Inc.—Carl Mydans/*Life* Magazine © Time Inc.; CORBIS (3). **93:** CORBIS—National Archives Neg. No. 208-PU-138LL-3—Oswald Wild/*Life* Magazine; CORBIS/Bettmann—CORBIS/Bettmann—U.S. Navy—CORBIS. **94, 95:** Harry S. Truman Library, Independence, Mo.; CORBIS/Bettmann. **96:** Bob Gomel/*Life* Magazine. **97:** CORBIS/Bettmann; Francis Miller/*Life* Magazine © Time Inc. **98, 99:** National Baseball Hall of Fame Library, Cooperstown, N.Y.; CORBIS/Bettmann. **100:** Air Force History Office, Edwards Air Force Base, Calif. **101:** © Arnold Newman, New York. **102:** CORBIS/Bettmann. **103:** Movie Still Archives, Harrison, Nebr. (2)—Archive Photos, New York; NBC/Globe Photos, New York—CORBIS/Bettmann—P. F. Bentley/Black Star, New York; Michael Ochs Archives, Venice, Calif. **104:** Rene Burri/Magnum Photos, Paris—Camera Press, London—Sovfoto, New York. **105:** Camera Press, London. **106:** CORBIS/Bettmann. **107:** CORBIS (3); Larry Burrows—Hulton Getty/Liaison Agency, New York—Ben Martin/*Time* Magazine. **108:** Cornell Capa/Magnum Photos, New York. **109:** Lisa Larsen/*Life* Magazine © Time Inc. **110:** Personality Photos, Inc., Brooklyn, N.Y. **111:** Philippe Halsman © Halsman Estate. **112:** CORBIS/Bettmann. **113:** CORBIS—Ben Carbonetto Collection—CORBIS—John Swope/*Life* Magazine © Time Inc.; CORBIS—CORBIS/Bettmann—Movie Still Archives, Harrison, Nebr., CORBIS/Bettmann. **114, 115:** Courtesy Doris Held, Cambridge, Mass. from *The Father of Spin* by Larry Tye © 1998 Larry Tye; Archive Photos, New York; AP/Wide World Photos. **116:** CORBIS/Bettman. **117:** The James Dean Memorial Gallery, Fairmount, Ind. **118:** Flip Schulke/Black Star, New York. **119:** Archive Photos, New York. **120:** CORBIS/Bettmann—Don Cravens/*Life* Magazine © Time Inc.—CORBIS—CORBIS/Bettmann; AP/Wide World Photos—CORBIS/Bettmann (2)—AP/Wide World Photos. **121:** CORBIS.

122: Charles Bonnay—John Bryson. 123: Jack Stager/Globe Photos, New York. 124: Alfred Eisenstaedt/*Life* Magazine © Time Inc. 125: Robert F. Sisson/National Geographic Society Image Collection, Washington, D.C.; no credit. 126: CORBIS—Library of Congress No. USZ C4-4-892—National Archives. 127: © 1999 Jacques Lowe, New York. 128: Luis Sanchez—Art Shay/*Life* Magazine © Time Inc. 129: © Erich Hartmann/Magnum Photos, New York. 130: From *Dylan: A Biography* by Bob Spitz, McGraw-Hill Publishing Company, © 1989 by Bob Spitz—Danny Lyon/Magnum Photos, New York. 131: Daniel Kramer, New York. 132: David Gahr. 133: Gordon Parks. 134: *Express Newspapers/Archive Photos, New* York. 135: Everett Collection/CSU Archives—John Giannini/Liaison Agency, New York; John Dominis/*Life* Magazine © Time Inc.—H. Kluetmeier/*Sports Illustrated*—George Tiedemann/*Sports Illustrated*—Tony Duffy/AllSport Photography, Pacific Palisades, Calif. 136, 137: Copyright Apple Corps Ltd., London. 138: CORBIS/Bettmann. 139: Marc Riboud/Magnum Photos, New York. 140: LBJ Library Collection, Austin, Tex. 141: Yoichi R. Okamoto, LBJ Library Collection, Austin, Tex. 142, 143: NASA; Lynn Pelham/*Life* Magazine © Time Inc. 144: CORBIS/Bettmann. 145: Eric Schweikardt/*Sports Illustrated;* Greg Gorman/Liaison Agency, New York. 146: Marianne Barcelona, New York; Mark Perlstein/Black Star, New York. 147: CORBIS/Bettmann; Hulton Getty/Liaison Agency, New York—Dilip Mehta/Contact Press Images, New York—Dennis Brack Ltd./Black Star, New York; Christopher Morris/Black Star, New York—Peter Smith/Liaison Agency, New York—Cindy Karp/Black Star, New York. 148: AP/Wide World Photos—CORBIS/Bettmann—National Archives Neg. No. 8525 #2. 149: Bill Pierce/*Time* Magazine. 150: Harry Coughanour—Neil Leifer, New York. 151: Ken Regan/Camera 5, New York. 152: CORBIS/Bettmann—Library of Congress—CORBIS/

Bettmann; Neil Leifer, New York—CORBIS/Bettmann—Neil Leifer, New York—Jerry Wachter/*Sports Illustrated*. 153: Courtesy Richard Y. Hoffman—courtesy Joel Finler, London. 154, 155: CORBIS/Bettmann. 156, 157: Photo courtesy Apple Computer, Inc.; David Burnett/Contact Press Images, New York; Raghu Rai/Magnum Photos, New York. 158: AP/Wide World Photos—Dennis Brack Ltd./Black Star, New York. 159: Pete Souza/White House/Liaison Agency, New York. 160: Rudy Frey/*Time* Magazine. 161: © 1991 David Burnett/Contact Press Images, New York. 162: Reprinted with permission, *Seattle Post-Intelligencer* © 1981; used by permission of Motown Record Company, L.P., a Universal Music Group Company. 163: Sam Emerson, Los Angeles, Calif. 164: NASA. 165: Greg English/Link Picture Library, London. 166: Michael O'Brien, Austin, Tex. 167: Hubbard/Liaison Agency, New York. 168: Terry Thompson/Sipa Press, New York. 169: CORBIS/Turnley Brothers. 170: AP/Wide World Photos. 171: David Burnett/Contact Press Images, New York. 172: Linda L. Creighton. 173: © Jonathan Becker/Liaison Agency, New York. 174: Dirk Halstead/*Time* Magazine. 175: Sergei Guneyev/*Time* Magazine; David Burnett/Contact Press Images, New York. 176: Agence France Presse Photo—Roger Sandler/Black Star, New York. 177: Cynthia Johnson, Washington, D.C. 178: James Keyser/*Time* Magazine; Barry von Below. 179: Peter Magubane/*Time* Magazine. 180: Ralf-Finn Hestoft/SABA Press Photos, New York—AP/Wide World Photos. 181: A. Berliner/Liaison Agency, New York; © Remi Benali/Liaison Agency, New York. 182: Patrick Lichfield/Camera Press, London—Jayne Fincher/Photographers International, Guildford, Surrey, England. 183: Tim Graham/Sygma, New York. 184: John Biever/*Sports Illustrated*. 185: Darryl Estrine/CORBIS/Outline Press; Shelly Katz/Gamma/Liaison Agency, New York. 186, 187: © Arnie Sachs/Sygma, New York; Diana Walker/*Time* Magazine.

BIBLIOGRAPHY

BOOKS
Addams, Jane. *Newer Ideals of Peace.* New York: Macmillan, 1907.
America A to Z. Pleasantville, N.Y.: Reader's Digest, 1997.
American Decades: 1940-1949. Ed. by Victor Bondi. Detroit: Gale Research, 1995.
Berle, Milton. *Milton Berle.* New York: Delacorte Press, [1974].
Beschloss, Michael R. *Eisenhower.* New York: HarperCollins, 1990.
Black Heroes of the 20th Century. Ed. by Jessie Carney Smith. Detroit: Visible Ink, 1988.
Bloom, Lynn Z. *Doctor Spock.* Indianapolis: Bobbs-Merrill, 1972.
Bullock, Alan. *Hitler.* New York: Harper & Row, [1971].
Cannon, Lou. *President Reagan.* New York: Simon & Schuster, 1991.
Castleman, Harry, and Walter J. Podrazik. *Watching TV.* New York: McGraw-Hill, 1982.
Celebrate the Century. Alexandria, Va.: Time-Life Books, 1998.
Cook, Blanche Wiesen. *Eleanor Roosevelt.* New York: Viking, 1992.
Dalton, Dennis. *Mahatma Gandhi.* New York: Columbia University Press, 1993.
Deutscher, Isaac. *Stalin.* London: Oxford University Press, 1967.
Dictionary of Scientific Biography (Vol. 2). Ed. by Charles Coulston Gillispie. New York: Charles Scribner's Sons, 1981.
Dupuy, Trevor Nevitt. *Combat Leaders of World War II* (Vol. 17 of *Military History of World War II*). New York: Franklin Watts, 1965.
Ellmann, Richard. *James Joyce.* New York: Oxford University Press, 1959.
Encyclopedia of American Biography. Ed. by John A. Garraty. New York: HarperCollins, 1996.
Encyclopedia of World Biography. Detroit: Gale Research, 1998.
Evans, Harold. *The American Century.* New York: Alfred A. Knopf, 1998.
Ewen, David. *George Gershwin.* Englewood Cliffs, N.J.: Prentice-Hall, [1970].
Facts On File Yearbook, 1941-1998. New York: Facts On File, 1942-1999.
Farrell, John C. *Beloved Lady.* Baltimore: Johns Hopkins Press, [1967].
Fischer, Daniel, and Hilmar Duerbeck. *Hubble.* Trans. by Helmut Jenkner and Douglas Duncan. New York: Copernicus, 1996.
Frank, Alan. *Marlon Brando.* New York: Exeter Books, 1982.
Freedman, Russell. *The Wright Brothers.* New York: Holiday House, 1991.
Freud, Ernst, Lucie Freud, and Ilse Grubrich-Simitis (eds.). *Sigmund Freud.* Trans. by Christine Trollope. New York: Harcourt Brace Jovanovich, 1976.
Friedan, Betty. *It Changed My Life.* Cambridge, Mass.: Harvard University Press, 1998.
Gilbert, Martin. *Churchill.* New York: Holt, 1991.
Great People of the 20th Century. New York: Time, 1996.
Greenfeld, Howard. *Caruso.* New York: G. P. Putnam's Sons, 1983.
Heilbrun, Carolyn G. *The Education of a Woman.* New York: Ballantine Books, 1995.
Hepburn, Katharine. *Me.* New York: Alfred A. Knopf, 1991.
Historic World Leaders (Vol. 2: *Europe, A-K*). Ed. by Anne Commire. Detroit: Gale Research, 1994.
Hixson, Walter L. *Charles A. Lindbergh.* Ed. by Oscar Handlin. New York: HarperCollins, 1996.
Horowitz, Daniel. *Betty Friedan and the Making of the Feminine Mystique.*

Amherst: University of Massachusetts Press, 1998.
Keller, Helen. *The Story of My Life.* New York: Laurel Leaf Library, 1961.
King, Norman. *Everybody Loves Oprah!.* New York: William Morrow, 1987.
Kobler, John. *Luce.* Garden City, N.Y.: Doubleday, 1968.
Lash, Joseph P. *Helen and Teacher.* New York: Delacorte Press, 1980.
Lear, Linda. *Rachel Carson.* New York: Henry Holt, 1997.
Lehman, Milton. *This High Man.* New York: Farrar, Straus, [1963].
Lloyd, Norman. *Encyclopedia of Music.* New York: Golden Press, 1968.
Love, Spencie. *One Blood.* Chapel Hill: University of North Carolina Press, 1996.
McCorvey, Norma. *I Am Roe.* New York: HarperCollins, 1994.
McCullough, David G. *Truman.* New York: Simon & Schuster, 1992.
McMurry, Linda O. *George Washington Carver.* New York: Oxford University Press, 1981.
Marconi, Degna. *My Father, Marconi.* New York: McGraw-Hill, 1962.
Mason, Francis. *I Remember Balanchine.* New York: Doubleday, 1991.
Maurois, André. *The Life of Sir Alexander Fleming.* Trans. by Gerard Hopkins. London: Jonathan Cape, 1959.
Mead, Margaret. *Blackberry Winter.* New York: Kodansha International, 1995.
Notable American Women: 1607-1950 (Vol. 1). Ed. by Edward T. James. Cambridge, Mass.: Belknap Press of Harvard University Press, 1971.
Notable Twentieth-Century Scientists (Vol. 3). Ed. by Emily J. McMurray. New York: Gale Research, 1995.
100 Greatest TV Shows of All Time. New York: Entertainment Weekly Books, 1998.
Our Times. Atlanta: Turner, 1995.
Patterson, James T. *Grand Expectations.* New York: Oxford University Press, 1996.
Payne, Tom. *Encyclopedia of Great Writers.* New York: Barnes & Noble, 1997.
Perry, Bruce. *Malcolm.* Barrytown, N.Y.: Station Hill Press, 1991.
Purcell, Hugh. *Mao Tse-tung.* New York: St. Martin's Press, 1977.
Rampersad, Arnold. *Jackie Robinson.* New York: Alfred A. Knopf, 1997.
Rees, Dafydd, and Luke Crampton. *Encyclopedia of Rock Stars.* New York: DK Publishing, 1996.
Roberts, Jack L. *Booker T. Washington.* Brookfield, Conn.: Millbrook Press, 1995.
Royal, Denise. *The Story of J. Robert Oppenheimer.* New York: St. Martin's Press, 1969.
Rubel, David. *Mr. President.* Alexandria, Va.: Time-Life Books, 1998.
Schorer, Mark. *Sinclair Lewis.* New York: McGraw-Hill, [1961].
Selden, Bernice. *The Story of Walt Disney.* Milwaukee: G. Stevens, 1996.
Sperber, A. M. *Murrow.* New York: Freundlich Books, 1986.
Spink, Kathryn. *Mother Teresa.* San Francisco: HarperCollins, 1997.
Trager, James. *The People's Chronology.* New York: Henry Holt, 1992.
Tutu, Desmond. *The Words of Desmond Tutu.* New York: Newmarket Press, 1989.
Tyson, Remer. *The Father of Spin.* New York: Crown Publishers, 1998.
Ward, Geoffrey C. *Baseball.* New York: Alfred A. Knopf, 1994.
Ware, Susan. *Letter to the World.* New York: W. W. Norton, 1998.
Washington, Booker T. *Up From Slavery.* New York: Penguin Books, 1986.
Watson, James D. *The Double Helix.* Ed. by Gunther S. Stent. New York: W. W. Norton, 1980.
Wechsler, James Arthur. *Labor Baron.* Westport, Conn.: Greenwood Press, [1972].
Wexler, Sanford. *The Civil Rights Movement.* New York: Facts On File, 1993.

White, G. Edward. *Earl Warren.* New York: Oxford University Press, 1982.
White, Ryan, and Ann Marie Cunningham. *Ryan White.* New York: Dial Books, 1991.
Williams, Juan. *Thurgood Marshall.* New York: Times Books, 1998.
Yeager, Chuck, and Leo Janos. *Yeager.* New York: Bantam Books, 1985.
Yeager, Chuck, et al. *The Quest for Mach One.* New York: Penguin, 1997.

PERIODICALS

"Artists and Entertainers of the Century." *Time,* June 8, 1998.
"Builders and Titans." *Time,* December 7, 1998.
"The Century's Greatest Minds." *Time,* March 29, 1999.
Drucker, Joel. "Billie Jean King." *Biography,* September 1998.
"Leaders and Revolutionaries." *Time,* April 13, 1998.
Life, 1936-1999.
People, 1974-January 1999.
Rompalske, Dorothy. "Princess Diana." *Biography,* September 1998.
Schueler, Donald G. "Inventor Marconi." *Smithsonian,* March 1982.
Scott, Cynthia. "Billie Jean King." *Contemporary Women's Issues,* March 1, 1997.
Solomon, Harvey. "Making Blockbusters, Billions, and Breakfast." *Biography,* March 1999.
Time, 1923-1999.

OTHER SOURCES

Academy of Achievement. Available: www.achievement.org. March 23, 1999.

Billy Graham Center Archives. Available: www.wheaton.edu/bgc/archives/archhp1.html
"Canada at War." *The Valour and the Horror.* Available: www.valourandhorror.com March 23, 1999.
Encyclopedia Britannica. Available: www.eb.com March 23, 1999.
ESPN SportsCentury. Available: http://espn.go.com/sportscentury/index.html
Labor Hall of Fame. Available: www.4better.com/laborhall March 23, 1999.
NASA Goddard Space Flight Center. Available: pao.gsfc.nasa.gov March 23, 1999.
National Baseball Hall of Fame and Museum. Available: www.baseballhalloffame.org March 23, 1999.
The Nobel Foundation. Available: www.nobel.se March 23, 1999.
Presidents of the United States. The Internet Public Library. Available: www.ipl.org/ref/POTUS/index.html
ScienceNet. Available: www.sciencenet.org.uk March 23, 1999.
Smithsonian Institution. Available: www.si.edu March 23, 1999.
Sports in the 20th Century. CBS SportsLine. Available: www.sportsline.com/u/century/index.html
United Mine Workers Association. Available: www.access.digex.-net.miner March 23, 1999.
Walter Reed Army Medical Center. Available: www.wramc.amedd.army.mil March 23, 1999.
"World War II Commemoration." *Grolier Interactive Online.* Available: gi.grolier.com/wwii/wwii_mainpage.html March 23, 1999.

INDEX

TIME® LIFE BOOKS

Time-Life Books is a division of Time Life Inc.

TIME LIFE INC.
PRESIDENT and CEO: George Artandi

TIME-LIFE BOOKS
PUBLISHER/MANAGING EDITOR: Neil Kagan
VICE PRESIDENT, MARKETING: Joseph A. Kuna
VICE PRESIDENT, NEW PRODUCT DEVELOPMENT: Amy Golden

OUR AMERICAN CENTURY

EDITORS: Loretta Britten, Paul Mathless
DIRECTOR, NEW PRODUCT DEVELOPMENT: Elizabeth D. Ward
DIRECTOR OF MARKETING: Pamela R. Farrell

People Who Shaped the Century
Deputy Editors: Kristin Hanneman (principal), Charles J. Hagner
Text Editors: Elizabeth Hedstrom, Stephen G. Hyslop, Karen Sweet
Associate Editors/Research and Writing: Barbara Reynolds Cather, Annette Scarpitta
Associate Marketing Manager: Terri Miller
Picture Associate: Anne Whittle
Senior Copyeditor: Anne Farr
Technical Art Specialist: John Drummond
Photo Coordinator: Betty H. Weatherley
Editorial Assistant: Christine Higgins

Design for **Our American Century** by Antonio Alcalá, Studio A, Alexandria, Virginia.

Special Contributors: Sarah Brash, Philip Brandt George (editing); Michael Blumenthal, Carol Brown, Janet Cave, George Constable, Ruth Goldberg, Mimi Harrison, Lee Hassig, Jim Hicks, James Michael Lynch, Janet Palmer Mullaney, Robert H. Wooldridge Jr. (writing); Constance Contreras, Robert Lee Hodge, Susan V. Kelly, Jane Martin, Elizabeth Thompson (research); Richard Friend, Marti Davila (design); Susan Nedrow (index).

Correspondents: Christine Hinze (London), Christina Lieberman (New York), Maria Vincenza Aloisi (Paris). Valuable assistance was also provided by Angelika Lemmer (Bonn).

Director of Finance: Christopher Hearing
Directors of Book Production: Marjann Caldwell, Patricia Pascale
Director of Publishing Technology: Betsi McGrath
Director of Photography and Research: John Conrad Weiser
Director of Editorial Administration: Barbara Levitt
Manager, Technical Services: Anne Topp
Senior Production Manager: Ken Sabol
Production Manager: Virginia Reardon
Quality Assurance Manager: James King
Chief Librarian: Louise D. Forstall

Separations by the Time-Life Imaging Department.

First printing. Printed in U.S.A.
School and library distribution by Time-Life Education, P.O. Box 85026, Richmond, Virginia 23285-5026.

EDITORIAL CONSULTANT
Richard B. Stolley is currently senior editorial adviser at Time Inc. After 19 years at *Life* magazine as a reporter, bureau chief, and assistant managing editor, he became the first managing editor of *People* magazine, a position he held with great success for eight years. He then returned to *Life* magazine as managing editor and later served as editorial director for all Time Inc. magazines. In 1997 Stolley received the Henry Johnson Fisher Award for Lifetime Achievement, the magazine industry's highest honor.

Other History Publications:

World War II
What Life Was Like
The American Story
Voices of the Civil War
The American Indians
Lost Civilizations
Mysteries of the Unknown
Time Frame
The Civil War
Cultural Atlas

Library of Congress Cataloging-in Publication Data
People who shaped the century / by the editors of Time-Life Books.
p. cm.—(Our American century)
Includes bibliographical references and index.
ISBN 0-7835-5513-X
1. Biography—20th century. 2. United States Biography.
I. Time-Life Books. II. Series.
CT120.P47 1999
920.009'04—dc21 99-25626
CIP

R 10 9 8 7 6 5 4 3 2 1

For information on and a full description of any of the Time-Life Books series listed above, please call 1-800-621-7026 or write:

Reader Information
Time-Life Customer Service
P.O. Box C-32068
Richmond, Virginia 23261-2068

On the cover:
Pestered constantly to pose for photographs, paintings, and sculptures, Albert Einstein, shown here in 1947, once jokingly gave his occupation as "artist's model." An often disheveled figure who went about engrossed in thought and detached from his surroundings, Einstein admitted, "I have never belonged wholeheartedly to country or state, to my circle of friends, or even to my own family." Pictured across the top of the cover are other memorable 20th-century personalities: Sigmund Freud, Dwight D. Eisenhower, Katharine Hepburn, John Lennon, Mother Teresa, and Michael Jordan. Martin Luther King Jr. is shown on the spine.